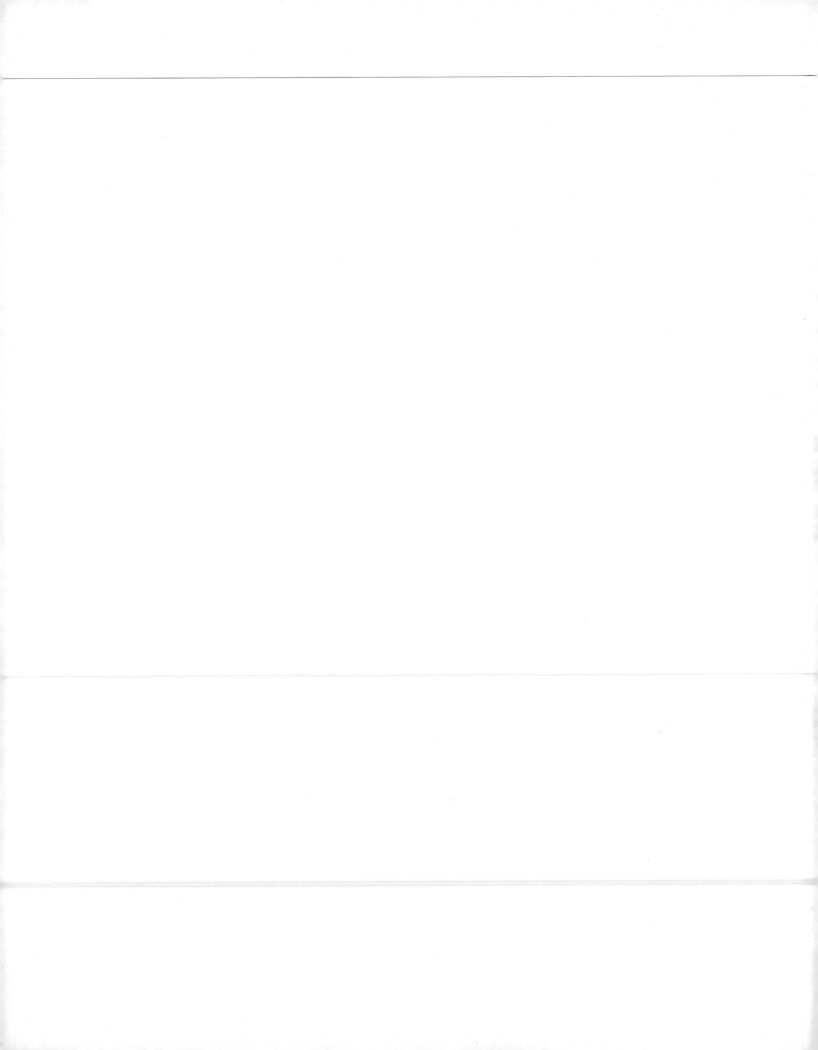

Cecil Hayes

CECIL HAYES
9 Steps to Beautiful Living

WATSON-GUPTILL PUBLICATIONS
New York

Senior Acquisitions Editor: Victoria Craven
Project Editor: Isabel Venero
Designer: Areta Buk/Thumb Print
Senior Production Manager: Ellen Greene

First published in the United States by
Watson-Guptill Publications
a division of VNU Business Media, Inc.
770 Broadway
New York, New York 10003
www.watsonguptill.com

Library of Congress Cataloging-in-Publication Data

Hayes, Cecil.
        Cecil Hayes 9 steps to beautiful living: dream, design, and decorate your home with style.
                p. cm.
        Includes index.
        ISBN 0-8230-0574-7
        1. Interior decoration—Handbooks, manuals, etc. I. Title: Cecil Hayes nine steps to beautiful living.
                II. Title: dream, design, and decorate your home with style. III. Title: 9 steps to beautiful
                living. IV. Title.
        NK2115.H36 2006
        747—dc22
        2005024087

Printed in China

First printing, 2006

1 2 3 4 5 6 7 8 9 / 14 13 12 11 10 09 08 07 06

I dedicate this book to my mom and dad, Edna and John Hayes, and my husband, Arzell Powell, for their loving support and belief in me; and to Mikala and Teandre for giving me faith in the future. I love you all very much.

And a special dedication to Tara Blackwell, my marketing director, whose writing and editing skills and passion for this subject gave me the confidence that the text presented here is clear and helpful to the do-it-yourself interior decorator.

Acknowledgments

This book couldn't have been created without the help of many, many people.

My clients, whose gift was entrusting me with their homes. Without them, there would be no nine-step process and certainly no way to express my art.

My family members, who represent the majority of my office staff, and whose hard work and dedication have helped me create the projects featured on these pages. Special thanks to my niece and office manager, Shea Burrows-Orgill, and my sister and accounting manager, Almedia Bannerman, for making my life run smoothly, keeping me organized, and always being willing to pitch in and help out no matter what the project. Because most of the furniture pieces in my interiors are my custom designs, a top manufacturing team is essential. The pencil can do great things, but it's the saw that turns those dreams into reality. My husband and my brother-in-law, Venus, are true master craftsmen. Without their skills, Cecil's Signature Furniture Collection would not have been possible, nor would the realization of my custom designs.

My editor, Victoria Craven, and all the staff at Watson-Guptill who have worked so hard on this manuscript. Thank you for giving me the chance to tell my story.

And finally, I wish to give special acknowledgment to Paige Rense, editor in chief of *Architectural Digest*. When I was first named to the Architectural Digest Top 100 (their list of the top 100 interior designers and architects in the world), Paige challenged the group of us to take our artistic talents to the next level. It is because of her encouragement that I began to think "outside the design box."

Contents

Introduction   8

Overview   12

STEP 1 Get to Know Your Space   15

STEP 2 Create Your Personal Look Book   37

STEP 3 Create a Furniture Plan   51

STEP 4 Decorate One Layer at a Time   69

STEP 5 Mix Styles and Periods   99

STEP 6 Choose Your Colors   111

STEP 7 Use a Variety of Fabric Patterns and Textures   127

STEP 8 Decorate with Art and Accessories   143

STEP 9 Evaluate Your Finished Design   161

Final Thoughts   170

Appendix: Standard Furniture Sizes   172

Sources   174

Photo Credits   175

Index   176

Introduction

OPPOSITE **As you will see throughout this book, I love to use throw pillows and other accessories on sofas. They can add accents of color or pattern and are very affordable.**

THIS BOOK WAS WRITTEN for the person who is passionate about great interior design. You know the one: the person who is an avid reader of design books and magazines, who spends countless hours pouring over their pages to glean any information and inspiration on how to put together one of those fabulous interiors for themselves, the person who wants his or her home to have a professionally designed look without the professionally designed price tag. This book is also for the many people who have seen my work featured in magazines and said, "I can't afford you, Cecil, but when I win the lottery, you'll be my first call." Well, even though your numbers didn't come up, I can still be your personal guide as you design your home and share with you all my secrets to beautiful living.

This book is *not* for people who want a one-day fix. And it certainly is not for people who let their neighbors come in and redecorate their homes! I won't teach you how to make crafts like painted boxes or needlepoint with the idea that this one element will transform your home into your dream space. What this book *will* do is show you the "how" and "why" of a successful interior design.

For those who have said to me over the years, "Oh, what you do must be so much fun," all I have to say is that "fun" for me is a day at the beach. Interior design is exciting and creative, but it is also hard work. The truth is that the interiors you admire so much in magazines and books might have taken several months to complete. They required lots of thoughtful consideration and planning on the part of many people. The reward of all this effort, however, is much more gratifying (and certainly more lasting) than any day at the beach.

When I decided to write this book, I knew I had to make it easy to understand for the non-professional. I've seen too many TV shows and read too many books that tried to explain not only how to decorate a home, but why various approaches to decorating worked. So much of the time, what they were advising didn't make sense, or worse yet, required the expertise of a professional. All their explanations of how to achieve a fantastic interior design left me with questions, some-times *lots* of questions. So, if any of you reading this book have been disappointed by others' attempts to give you a logical and understandable approach to interior design, you aren't alone. This book gives you just that: an easy-to-follow nine-step process that I have developed and perfected over many years.

When I first founded my interior design company, my dealings with clients were very hard on my ego. They questioned every selection I made, and I felt like I was always on the defensive. I knew I was making the right choices for their home, but I always had to convince them of it. I know now there was a good reason things weren't going according to plan: my approach was all wrong.

In the early days, Step 1 of my process involved taking my client shopping. In fact, I followed clients' leads about where to shop. These shopping trips were not productive at all. We went all over town, looked at scores of items, and at the end of the day, we were no closer to narrowing down what we wanted. On these trips, no one was in control of the project—not the client and not me.

In some instances a client had a vision of the finished project, which you would think would make the process easier. On the contrary: with a fairly well-developed idea already, it became nearly impossible to dissuade him or her from pursuing a design that I knew would not give the desired result.

I was at an impasse: every project I was doing was taking unproductive detours and ultimately I wasn't happy and neither were some of my clients. I was so discouraged I was thinking about returning to my original profession as an art teacher and artist, when finally, all of a sudden, I came up with a plan of how to approach my work. I realized that it wasn't the client's job to create a vision based on a few visits to stores—that was my job. I needed to present to the client my ideas with an organized plan. I would offer them a few choices—based on my initial selections—and *then* they could make decisions about decorative items.

This was the genesis of my nine-step process. By developing these steps, I not only created some much needed structure in my approach, I changed the way clients viewed—and accepted—my ideas and expertise. I truly believe that my nine-step process is the reason my clients think creating a gorgeous interior is fun. And I agree with them: it is fun for the client. As I said earlier, the designer has to do a lot of hard work in order for the client to have fun. So, since you are about to become both the designer and the client, don't expect everything to be fun.

Think about it like this: you're having a dinner party. Your guest list includes 25 of your closest friends. Since you are the host, you are doing the shopping, cooking, and decorating. Finally, the day arrives, your guests come, and everyone enjoys the fruits of your labor. The food is delicious, the table setting is divine, and the company is better still. As the guests leave, they tell you what a wonderful time it's been, and their compliments make all of your hard work seem worthwhile. But the truth is that the hours leading up to the party were not always stress-free.

Interior design is very similar. There will be days and weeks when it will be so frustrating and so much work that you'll wish you'd never started. But once the job is done, and you've been able to realize your vision and transform a space that is simply satisfactory to one that is stupendous, you can't imagine how rewarding it will be. So, read this book—every step—and I will teach you the tips and techniques I have learned over the many years I have been an interior designer. I promise you it will be one of the most gratifying endeavors you have ever undertaken.

Love,

Ceil

P.S. If you do win the lottery, don't read the book—call me!

BELOW **I've used a mixture of textures to create interest in my home, including leather, stone, metal, wood, silk, glass, and tile. Although there are touches of color in the artwork, the color flow comes from the chocolate brown and black used throughout the rooms.**
PHOTOGRAPHY BY KIM SARGENT. COURTESY ARCHITECTURAL DIGEST. ©2004. THE CONDÉ NAST PUBLICATIONS, INC. ALL RIGHTS RESERVED. USED WITH PERMISSION.

OPPOSITE **This amply sized dining room is perfect for a large gathering of friends and family. I used light neutrals on the walls and upholstery so the deep, rich color of the rococo-inspired wood table and chairs, ornate light fixture, and painting were well showcased.**

Overview

BEFORE YOU GET STARTED, here is a quick overview of what each of the nine steps will teach you.

STEP 1 Get to Know Your Space

To begin the process of designing your home, you need to know what's in it first. This step will guide you through taking a closer look at your space to determine several elements or features that will impact your finished decor, including: light levels, what kind of view you have (interior or exterior), and how your room(s) will be used. I will also show you how to take measurements of your room and create a floor plan that indicates structural and mechanical items (such as air conditioning and heating vents and electrical outlets).

STEP 2 Create Your Personal Look Book

A "Look Book" is a portfolio that you put together containing clippings from magazines of designs you'd like to emulate in your home, as well as photographs taken on shopping trips of decorative items you want in your finished design. In this chapter, I will show you how to organize your Look Book and advise you on what is essential to include. When it's completed, it will be an invaluable guide as you make decisions about furnishings, art, and accessories for your new decor.

The wood cabinetry in medium tones in this kitchen and breakfast room give the space a stately yet warm feel. Beautiful details such as the crown molding, chair rail, and decorative arch give definition to the room.

STEP 3 Create a Furniture Plan

A furniture arrangement—or what I call a "furniture plan"—should be functional and comfortable. In addition, the proportional relationships between individual pieces of furniture must be correct, so that the ensemble looks good in the space it occupies. In this chapter, I will provide you with the necessary information to create a furniture plan that enhances your room.

STEP 4 Decorate One Layer at a Time

To make the design process easier, I have formulated a "ratio recipe" that spells out what percentage of the total number of decorative items gets divided among the three areas, or layers, in a room, which are the floor, the walls, and the ceiling. With this ratio recipe, it is much easier to make decisions about how many items should be part of your decor, as well as to make decisions regarding how much of your total budget is allocated to purchases for each layer.

STEP 5 Mix Styles and Periods

While many of us like the look created by decorating with furnishings and accessories of the same style, there are many others who like to mix styles and periods in a decor. Generally, there are two personality types who like the latter approach: the "collector" and the "eclectic." If one of these types describes you, I will offer you advice on how to decorate your home that is specific to each approach.

STEP 6 Choose Your Colors

The power of color in a home cannot be underestimated: it is one of the most important features of any interior design. In this chapter, I encourage you to think about moving away from neutral color schemes and explain why I think color has a place in your decor. I will give you valuable information on how certain colors affect our moods and behavior, as well as share my rules for creating proper color balance and distribution in a room.

STEP 7 Use a Variety of Fabric Patterns and Textures

Creating a decor that is rich with different patterns and textures can be intimidating for the beginner, but in this chapter I offer you simple advice on how to do this successfully.

STEP 8 Decorate with Art and Accessories

Art and accessories play a vital role in achieving an interior design that looks finished and refined. In this chapter, I provide you with information about the many types of art and accessories and how to use them in your decor.

STEP 9 Evaluate Your Finished Design

In this final, important step, I guide you through making an honest assessment of how well you accomplished your goal of creating a beautifully designed home.

In Step 7, I will show you how to combine different patterns in your decor, as in this living room where floral drapes and throw pillows are paired with a striped sofa, all of which feature the same colors.

Get to Know Your Space

With the ever-increasing cost

of houses, it's more important than ever to know the space you live in. I know what you are thinking: "Of course I know my space. I live, sleep, and eat there every day!" But you'd be surprised by how many people, regardless of how long they have lived in their homes, aren't well acquainted with all of the elements of their space.

Why is knowing your space so important? You can't begin the process of designing (or redesigning) your home until you are familiar with all the aspects of the space that will affect the end result. In short, this information will lay the foundation for your finished interior design.

Think of the room(s) you plan to decorate like an unclothed body. We shop for clothes that complement our shape because we know our bodies. The same is true of our home decor: we need to keep in mind the specific details of our room—both structural and mechanical, such as the location of fixtures and electrical outlets, the amount of natural or artificial light, exact measurements—before we attempt to decorate it. And just as most people don't have a perfect body, most rooms in our homes are not our ideal space. One of my best friends wears a size 18, but when she pulls an outfit together, she looks better than most women half her size! The moral of the story: you need to work with what you have by understanding what you are working with, and when you do, the results can be fabulous. In today's marketplace the options are infinite—home decor stores have so much available to suit a wide range of needs—so whether you have a rustic house in the country or a modern loft in the city, you'll find furnishings, art, and accessories that will look like they were tailor-made for your space.

OPPOSITE **In this contemporary design, neutral furnishings and wallcoverings ensure that my client's extraordinary art collection is the main focus of the decor.**

So, let's get started. Walk around your room(s) several times, and take note of everything you see. You may think that you will know all the features of your room at a quick glance but, take it from a pro, **there are always things right in front of you that you didn't notice.** I promise you that after you walk through the space a few times it will become more like a game of "seek and find"! I can hear you now: "I didn't see that yesterday," or "I never noticed that the light switch is in the middle of the wall."

I could write an entire chapter just recounting the stories of the many, many times I didn't scrutinize a space closely enough and the trouble that this got me in. The majority of my business is devoted to creating custom furniture. In the first few years of my career, I would finish a piece and try to install it, only to discover I couldn't because of something like the location of a structural element that I should have taken into consideration. I spent a lot of time making adjustments that would have been unnecessary if I had just looked more closely. Now I have eyes like a frog that look in all directions!

Assess Existing Light Levels

ONE OF THE FEATURES that will have a big effect on any room is light exposure. Walk through your room several times at different times of the day. Does it have lots of natural light or is it dark? A bright space can be an asset, since good exposure from windows and skylights contributes to the open, airy feel of a space. Don't be concerned if your space is dark, you can always bring in more light (thank you, Thomas Edison!). In fact, low light levels can be worked to your advantage. Light—or lack of it—can be used to create a mood.

For a house with lots of windows and a beautiful view, the rooms will look very different during the day (opposite) and night (below), and when decorating around a view, you must keep this in mind. Note how the black wall coupled with the mica buffet and lacquered chairs create a different mood in these rooms after dark.

The combination of large picture windows and skylights in the sitting room of this New York brownstone makes it feel larger than it is.

The rooms that need to be lit well are the "working" rooms—bathrooms, closets, kitchens, and dining areas. Function is of paramount importance here, and light levels play a huge role in determining functionality. These are areas where colors need to be crisp and pure, where you need to be certain that what you see is what you get, and where adequate task lighting is a necessity. Proper lighting accurately reflects skin tones and color variations in clothing (a big help when you are trying to get dressed).

In the bathroom, good lighting is necessary over the sink or vanity, and fluorescents are an excellent choice. Select the full spectrum type if possible, because the warm overtones of these new fluorescent tubes resemble natural daylight. They're a little more expensive than standard

Cecil Says

I recommend carrying a notebook with you at all times during the "getting to know your space" step. If you jot notes to yourself along the way, you will be certain to remember every last detail. There are lots of them, and it may be nearly impossible to keep them in mind if you don't write them down.

fluorescent fixtures, but they eliminate the unflattering, harsh light most people associate with traditional fluorescents. They may actually change the way you feel about using this type of lighting in your home.

I recommend using fluorescent lighting in the closet as well. It has the benefit of even light distribution, it stays cool when in use (safety is important when adding light to a closet full of potentially flammable clothing), and it provides good light in a space that tends to be very dark.

In the kitchen, lighting takes several forms and includes ceiling lights for ambient lighting (such as recessed, track, or fluorescent lights) and under-cabinet lights for task-oriented activities. A combination of the two will probably serve you best. Most of you will find that you don't have enough under-cabinet lighting. It's amazing the difference it can make to a kitchen, but most people don't realize how much they need it until they finally install it. Food looks and, amazingly, tastes better in good lighting. Better lighting won't make you a Cordon Bleu chef, but it will make the process of cooking easier.

Adequate lighting is essential in any kitchen. In football star Ty Law's home, the open floor plan filters lots of ambient light into the kitchen, but I also added under-cabinet task lighting.

BATHROOM LIGHTING I believe that it is essential to use lightbulbs with a spectrum that approximates natural daylight in the bathroom. This is especially important in any area where you are dressing, putting on makeup, or performing any kind of grooming. Use color-corrected fluorescent tubes, color-corrected bulbs (such as **GE**'s Reveal), and halogen high-hats for the best-quality light.

ABOVE In this master bath, lighting is provided with fluorescent tubes concealed in the soffit. My clients are avid collectors of Southwestern art and the color scheme of turquoise, peach, and rust was inspired by the art in their home.

OPPOSITE, TOP **Elegant wall sconces are paired with high-hats, or ceiling lights, to provide much-needed task lighting in this master bathroom. I achieved the glamorous 1930s Hollywood look by using mirrored surfaces with the silver-leaf cabinetry. The glass knobs and countertops add another reflective element to further enhance the overall design.**

OPPOSITE, BOTTOM **This small bathroom relies on high-hat lights concealed in the soffit above the mirror for task lighting and the glass brick for additional diffused ambient light.**

This dining room demonstrates the proper relationship between the table height and the lighting fixture. There is ample room for the centerpiece—which includes a pair of temple dogs—but the chandelier is low enough to provide the necessary illumination.

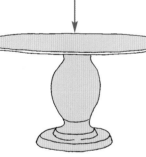

Dining table fixtures should be hung no more than 3 feet above the tabletop.

Dining areas and breakfast rooms also need good lighting, and a hanging fixture will provide the best source of light. The fixture should be located approximately 3 feet above the tabletop, and its placement should correspond to the center of the table.

You have probably noticed that dining room fixtures tend to be hung in the center of the room. The architect or contractor selects this spot because it is the best location for most furniture arrangements in that room. But you are creating a custom interior decor, so once you have determined your room layout, you may find that the location of the fixture is not centered over the dining table. If this is the case, it's a simple, inexpensive process to have the fixture moved, and I recommend that you do. We'll talk more about balance later in the book, but for now suffice it to say that centering the lighting fixture over the table will make the space more balanced. One final note about relocating fixtures: light fixtures in bathrooms, closets, kitchens, and dining rooms are usually attached to structural elements. When making changes in these areas, it's always best to hire an electrician, as this is no job for a novice.

While light levels are more critical in working rooms, they are important in other rooms as well. Lack of light in the nonworking rooms (bedrooms, living rooms, family rooms, and studies) is easily overcome through the use of floor lamps, table lamps, and wall lights. In other words, if you don't have enough light, plug more in! The thoughtful placement of additional fixtures in these rooms can enhance or create a variety of moods. When adding additional illumination, bear in mind that tall table lamps illuminate a room better than short lamps. For the best results, I recommend that table lamps be at least 2 feet tall.

With a huge variety of lightbulbs available now, you can control very precisely the kind of light you have in any room. You will want brighter, crisper light in kitchens, bathrooms, and closets and softer light in family and living rooms and bedrooms.

There are many types of lightbulbs to choose from that give off different kinds of light. For example, halogen bulbs give off a whiter, brighter light than incandescent bulbs, the ones commonly used in residential settings. The drawback is that they burn hotly and can burn you if you touch them when they are on. Incandescent bulbs have continued to evolve over recent years. In addition to the warm, slightly yellow glow familiar to most of us, they now come in many colors and finishes.

I prefer table lamps to be at least 2 feet tall for the best illumination. I chose this striking crystal lamp for my client who loves to read in bed.

Not only can you still find GE's Soft White bulb (an old standby), but the company also offers other choices, including Soft Pink (which is more flattering to skin tones). Other options are energy-saving Spiral and Biax compact fluorescent bulbs (guaranteed to last for four to eight years depending upon bulb type) and the new Reveal bulb (designed to more closely approximate natural daylight). I prefer the versatility of three-way bulbs, and I use them frequently in the houses I design. Typically, they illuminate at 60, 75, and 100 watts. With a flip of a switch, you can create three distinct moods with the same fixture.

Controlling the amount of light coming into a room is most often an issue in the bedroom. If you have a bedroom that receives light in the morning, use black out window treatments to ensure the sun streaming in in the morning doesn't disturb your sleep. This type of window treatment comes with a lining that completely blocks out light. If you want to filter the light rather than block it entirely, I suggest Hunter-Douglas's Duette and Silhouette brand.

For those of you in the enviable position of being able to determine how many windows you have because you are building your house or renovating, add as many windows as possible so that natural sunlight can brighten your space. Within the last 50 years, families have begun to spend more time indoors than at any other time in our history, so it's important that the time spent inside is as pleasant as possible. And, in my opinion, good light brings a lot of joy into a space.

Do You Have a View?

IF THERE IS SOMETHING BEAUTIFUL to look at beyond the four walls of your room and it gives you pleasure, you have a view. Your view can be a body of water, a wooded lot, snowcapped mountains, a manicured garden, or an impressive cityscape. Whatever it is, you'll want to make the most of it.

When designing your space around a view, keep in mind that the seating arrangement should always focus on it. This doesn't mean that every chair in the room should *face* the view. After all, you want a comfortable living area, not a theater! What you will need to do is work out a seating arrangement that showcases your view, but remains functional for your lifestyle.

I had a client with a magnificent ocean view that she wanted all her guests to appreciate, so she had all the seating facing that view. She thought it was a terrific idea, but in fact there were a few problems with this.

Furniture needs to be arranged for conversation, and if everybody is facing the window, it tends to make it difficult to talk to one another comfortably. The other problem was that my client was rarely at home during the day. Most of her entertaining was done during the evening. What she forgot to consider is that at night that beautiful view of the ocean completely vanished—her view became a big, black expanse. To avoid this or a similar situation in your house, remember not to let any one item—a view, a piece of furniture, or work of art—dictate the arrangement of your furnishings to the exclusion of everything else.

BELOW **If you're lucky enough to have a view like this one, you should emphasize it when you design your space. Using a piece of furniture that only partially obscures the window, like the leather daybed here, will not compete with the view.**

OPPOSITE **In this home, the interior view is the atrium filled with different types of beautiful plants and flowers, which you can see through this opening in the wall of the dining room.**

Cecil Says

If necessary, it is fine to place furnishings in front of the view window, but make sure the item is no more than 30–36 inches high. The furniture is still below eye level and doesn't detract from the view.

While an exterior view is always an attractive feature, you can certainly have a great space without it. If you like the idea of a view, you can create an interior "view," or focal point, for your room. This can be accomplished in a few ways: with a trompe l'oeil (literally "fool the eye") design or mural, an atrium, a collection of houseplants, a water feature such as a fountain or an aquarium, or a work of art. I've found that a large, well-lit painting with a subject you enjoy is an ideal focal point.

Another focal point many of you have already is a fireplace. The hearth wall and mantle naturally draw the eye, and many people arrange their rooms around it. Nothing compares to a crackling fire for creating a feeling of coziness.

Don't despair if your room does not have an exterior view, because creating an interior "view," or focal point, can be as simple as adding a beautiful art work that commands attention, either for the wall or the floor, or adding an aquarium with brightly colored fish and accessories.

RIGHT **This homeowner used a large oil painting to create an interior view. The serene garden scene is the next best thing to a real garden view.**

OPPOSITE **This unique metal fireplace with an enamel finish and large stone base is a wonderful built-in interior view.**

Determine How Your Room Will Be Used

TAKE A MOMENT TO JOT DOWN your plans for the room you are planning to decorate. Rooms may be used for as many purposes as families have needs. And just because a room was originally intended as a formal dining room, for example, doesn't mean that you have to use it as one.

During my career I've seen many creative uses of space. One of my bachelor clients chose to turn his dining room into a spectacular billiard room (men just love their toys!). Other clients have requested that the bedroom double as a workout area. But a creative use of space isn't limited to a large room. It can just as easily be a closet that has been transformed into an art niche or recessed bar. The options are only limited by your own imagination.

There is one trend, however, that does trouble me: the demise of the living room. I've met many people who question its importance. Clients often say "Nobody ever uses it" or "It feels like a museum," and they believe that the space could be put to much better use. I totally disagree.

The living room is the embodiment of your good taste and an introduction to your style for anyone who visits your home. It may not get much use, but it does make a fantastic impression, and designing the home of your dreams is very much about making an impression. So before you put that formal living room to another use, take a moment to think about what you will be missing without it. And remember that a beautiful room can still serve your needs and be durable if you make the right decisions for furnishings, upholstery, and floor coverings.

Planning is essential as you begin the process of designing your home, and taking the time *now* to anticipate how the space will be used will save you time and effort in the future.

BELOW **A living room is frequently your guests' first introduction to your style. In this one, it's evident the owner is a devoted collector of art and artifacts from around the world.**

OPPOSITE **Don't feel as though you must use a room for its originally intended purpose: in this foyer, I transformed an extra closet into a handsome wet bar.**

ABOVE **This home theater began as a larger-than-average guest bedroom on the second floor of my client's home. With the addition of stainless steel columns, theater seating, and a large projection system with surround sound, it is the perfect place to view a movie.**

RIGHT **What can you do with a small 12-by-12-foot guest room? My celebrity client chose to transform it into his home office. His desk, which I designed and created, is inscribed with Egyptian hieroglyphics chosen by him because of their spiritual meaning.**

PHOTOGRAPHY BY DAN FORER.
COURTESY ARCHITECTURAL DIGEST.
©1997. THE CONDÉ NAST
PUBLICATIONS, INC. ALL RIGHTS
RESERVED. USED WITH PERMISSION.

Measure Your Room

I CANNOT EMPHASIZE ENOUGH how important having accurate measurements of your space is to a successful interior design. *This is the single most important piece of information you will need.* You won't be able to make the right choices regarding your furnishings, floor coverings, and accessories without knowing the exact measurements of your room. Having this information on hand will prevent costly mistakes.

After I graduated from design school, I worked for a small interior design company. To this day I refer to that office as the "Sofa Burial Ground." The owner believed in "eye-balling" a space rather than taking measurements. Unfortunately, many times he missed important details like door openings and other structural elements. As a result, many of the sofas he chose were simply too large to fit in the space, and he had to absorb the cost of these mistakes. Since then, I have understood the absolute necessity of proper measurements.

There are two methods for measuring your space: "pacing off" the space or using a tape measure. While I prefer the latter method, you can get a reliable estimate by pacing off your room. To do so, place heel to toe as you walk across the floor. Each foot length is approximately equivalent to 1 foot. Having this estimate will avoid the misjudgments like the ones made by my former employer, but be aware that it will not be 100 percent accurate.

As a professional interior designer, I always use a tape measure. If you don't already have one, buy at least a 12-foot tape measure at your local home improvement store.

Whatever method you choose, be sure to take measurements not only of the floor but also of the height and length of the walls and all doors and windows. Record the measurements in feet and inches as opposed to just inches (i.e., 6'10" not 82"). Once you've completed your measurements, transfer this information to a floor plan. I can hear some of you right now saying "Cecil, I don't know how to make a floor plan!" Not to worry, I'm about to show you how.

Many homes feature "forgotten" spaces that can be put to good use, like the area under a staircase. Here an antique piano looks like it was tailor-made for the space underneath a spiral staircase.

Make a Floor Plan

A FLOOR PLAN REPRESENTS the floor view of a room. Most floor plans are either square or rectangular, but there are exceptions. Professional designers and architects use an architectural scale to create accurate, scaled-down replicas of rooms from these measurements. If you know how to make one, by all means do. For the beginner, however, a freehand drawing works just as well. I suggest you buy quarter-inch graph paper at an office supply or art store. Sketch your floor plan using a scale: one graph square should equal 1 foot.

A floor plan is absolutely essential as you begin to design your home, and you will be referring to it routinely throughout the process. In addition to the room's measurements, it should indicate the location of doors, windows, structural elements, such as columns, and any mechanical items.

The time you spend creating an accurate floor plan will be time well spent, because you will refer to it frequently. It is the next best thing to being able to fold up your room and take it with you when shopping for furnishings and decorative items.

Begin by drawing the shape of the room on the graph paper. Near the line for each wall, transfer its measurements. Indicate the size and location of doors and windows with open or broken lines. For doors, note how far the door swings into a room. (Refer to the diagram at left for guidance.) Make sure your drawing also contains the location and measurement of items you don't plan to move. These might include stairs, structural columns, light switches, air conditioning and heating vents, vacuum outlets, electrical outlets, alarm pads, and fireplaces. Also include the height of the ceiling. If in doubt about whether a feature's measurements and location should be noted, you should record the information. It's better to have too much information than too little.

Think of your floor plan as your primary design tool. Once it's completed, compare it to your list of possible uses for the space and look for potential areas of concern: for example, low ceilings, narrow doors, awkward door swings, and too few electrical outlets. These things may not pose problems in themselves, but if they interfere with how you intend to use the space, they need to be dealt with.

Even as a seasoned designer, I routinely go through every part of the process mentioned above and wouldn't consider designing a room without doing so. In fact, skipping any part of Step 1 would be like going on a road trip without a map. Imagine it: you're in an unfamiliar place. You have a goal in mind—a destination—and you eventually get there, but odds are it wasn't an easy trip without a map to help show the way. At the end of your trip, your journey will have been twice as long as necessary, cost twice as much as planned, and been fraught with stressful situations. The other option is to use your road map, plan well, and not waste time or money. The choice is yours.

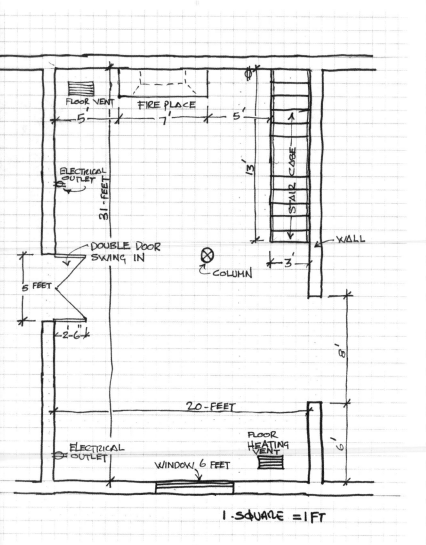

When I designed this room, the imposing stone fireplace was a feature I had to design around. With some creativity and planning, I was able to turn it into a focal point that my clients loved.

Let's Review

Getting to know your home is the first step in designing your space. Here's a recap of what you need to do to accomplish this.

1 **ASSESS EXISTING LIGHT LEVELS** Walk through your space at different times of the day and make note of light levels. You should have enough lighting to comfortably perform your daily tasks, particularly in working rooms.

2 **DO YOU HAVE A VIEW?** A room can have an exterior view or interior view. An interior view is a focal point and can include anything from a fireplace to a work of art.

3 **DETERMINE HOW YOUR ROOM WILL BE USED** Make a list of all the activities that will take place in the room, and decide how it will be used.

4 **MEASURE YOUR ROOM** Accurate measurements are essential to designing your home. By taking the time at this stage to get the proper measurements, you will save time and money in the long run, as you will avoid choosing furnishings and floor coverings in the wrong size.

5 **MAKE A FLOOR PLAN** A floor plan is a graphic representation of your room on paper, on which you will note measurements and the location of structural and mechanical elements.

Create Your Personal Look Book

A "Look Book" is a photo album of rooms and decorative items that appeal to you and that you have collected for decorating inspiration. I call it a "Look Book" because you'll look at scores of interior design magazines until one day your eyes will open wide, your finger will point, and you'll exclaim: "This is my look!" Needless to say, developing a Look Book is a fun and exciting process. Once it's completed, it will be a guide to your style preferences, which will help make shopping much easier. In putting it together, you will gain valuable insight into your likes and dislikes and understand what defines your look.

To begin creating your Look Book, you need to gather all the decorating magazines you've been saving and start ripping out pages that feature decors you like. Cut out anything that appeals to you, and don't worry about having too many examples; you can always edit these selections later. During this process, you will begin to identify your taste. It's time to move on from the "it will do" decor that you currently have in your home, to one that reflects who you are and enhances your lifestyle.

I must admit that this step was not part of my original process. In fact, I felt insulted when clients brought in photos of other designers' work. But I soon realized that these photos were not meant to be copied, but rather to serve as inspiration and provide insight into my clients' tastes. I am now in the position where clients tear out pages of *my* work from magazines and express how much they love the look!

OPPOSITE **An example of a Look Book with lots of clippings from magazines for inspiration, photos of items you want to include in your home, and a floor plan.**

Look for Inspiration

WHEN YOU BEGIN TO LOOK through the decorating magazines, be sure to select pictures of *entire* rooms that appeal to you. This is important because you are interested in the space overall, not just one element of it, and that's what you should focus on at this stage (I will talk about collecting photos of individual decorative items later). When you find a room that you really love, tear out the picture and study it. As you look at it, take note of all the details and how the designer makes use of space. If the room is designed well (and it most likely is if you are drawn to it), it has good balance and flow. I will use both of these terms throughout the book, so it's important that you understand what they mean. If all the elements in a composition (that is, the room and its contents) work together as an ensemble and have the proper proportions in relation to each other and the room, the room has balance. Color balance is slightly different, and it entails using the appropriate number of colors in the right "amount" (never too much of any one color). Flow refers to the effect created when there is continuity between features in a room (which is oftentimes created by using the same color or colors on several elements).

Take an even closer look at the photograph. The room should also have certain elements that are prominently displayed or emphasized in some way. These elements—what I call "featured items"—are focal points and style-setting accents. A featured item can be:

- Color
- Fabric
- Furniture
- Art
- Window treatment
- View
- Structural feature

With a sticky note, indicate on the photo what you feel are the featured items in the room. These items are important because many times they set the tone for the design. They may have been what drew your eye to the room's design in the first place.

BELOW **Many people prefer a more formal living room, such as this one, which features a large, skirted ottoman and an oversize gilded mirror framed by decorative molding set against a dramatic wall of windows.**

OPPOSITE, TOP **My family room exudes a feeling of warmth by using a combination of natural materials, including wood, leather, and grass cloth. The African art and accessories add texture and color.**

OPPOSITE, BOTTOM **This large, contemporary master bedroom and sitting area is decorated with Southwestern art and accessories.**

Studies can feel too sober because of the formality of the richly colored paneled walls and period furnishings, so it's important to create a space that is comfortable and inviting, as I did here by adding an antique recliner.

ACCEPT YOUR SPACE

By now you know the size of your room and you are familiar with its architectural features. Keep this in mind when you are looking through design magazines for inspiration. For your Look Book, only select photos of spaces the same size as your own. If your room measures 14 by 14 feet with a ceiling height of 9 feet, a photo of a room twice the size will not serve its intended purpose for the Look Book, which is to be a very close approximation of what you want to achieve in your space. The charm and great style of a room has nothing to do with its size. With thoughtful planning and patience, beautiful results are always possible regardless of the size of the room. Think about it this way: I love looking at fashion magazines to see how to dress myself. There are countless ideas, but so few people actually look like the models who fill those magazines. How many of us wear a size four? Not me! But I have found that, by keeping my size in mind along with an idea of how I want to look, I can find an ensemble that suits my body and looks fabulous.

If the style of the room you find for your Look Book doesn't fit your lifestyle, resist the temptation to use it as a model for your space. No matter how beautiful it is, designing a room that doesn't meet your needs ultimately won't make you happy.

ABOVE **This intimate dining room seats six people, unlike the larger dining room at left, and is the typical size found in condos and apartments. When choosing inspiration photos for your Look Book, be sure to include rooms that are nearly the same size as the ones you plan to design.**

LEFT **For this dining room—which can seat 12 guests—I carried aspects of the romantic decor from other parts of the house: I used soft colors on the walls, patterned upholstery for the chairs, dramatic candelabras, and a chandelier to complement the French furnishings in the other rooms.**

IT'S ALL IN THE DETAILS

Once you have all of the photos of the rooms you want, you can concentrate on looking for photos of detail and specialty items. These are small features that are part of larger items, such as a tassle on the end of a window shade cord, and they add a bit of ornament to enhance the appeal of an item. Choose photos that give you a close-up view of pattern, finish, and colors, so that you can have as much information as possible before making your final selection. Truly successful interior design is about paying attention to details, and sometimes small specialty items will be just the thing to embellish an otherwise ordinary item. Detail and specialty items include:

- Plumbing fixtures
- Tile/stone edging
- Molding
- Hardware for cabinets
- Window treatment accessories
- Trims on pillows or upholstery
- Nailheads

ABOVE **Details can be used to coordinate elements in a decor, such as in this traditional dining room. The red-checkered fabric on the chair on the right is used to trim the edges and buttons of the patterned upholstery on the chair on the left.**

RIGHT **Details like the carved corbels and subtle gilding add just the right amount of ornament to this bathroom vanity.**

Small details can make a major difference in the look of any decorative item. The pattern on this cornice treatment above the sliding glass doors was created by using brass nailheads, which pair beautifully with the grass cloth covering. When compiling your Look Book, be sure to include photos of details like these.

SHOP FOR IDEAS

The final pages of each section devoted to a specific room in your Look Book will feature photos of decorative items (furniture, accessories, etc.) gathered during research shopping trips. That's right, *research* shopping trips. These are specifically intended for getting more ideas and not about buying anything, so put away the checkbook.

There are three very good reasons why it's important to do research first and make purchases later:

1 **DESIGNING YOUR HOME SHOULD NOT BE UNDULY INFLUENCED BY THE LATEST TRENDS** Your decor could last a lifetime, or at least a very long time. Since that's the case, doesn't it make sense to spend time getting the right look?

2 **THE AVERAGE PERSON HAS NOT SHOPPED FOR FURNISHINGS IN YEARS** A research shopping trip is a chance to find out what's available in the marketplace and how much you'll have to spend to get the look you want.

3 **DECORATING IS AN INVESTMENT** The total cost to decorate the average home is approximately 20–25 percent of its value. This means that decorating your home, like purchasing it, is an investment that is best made after much thought and consideration.

RIGHT **In this rustic kitchen, the focal points are the back-splash, created from a variety of ceramic tiles in earth tones, and the big copper sink.**

OPPOSITE, TOP **Choose items with trims and fringe for added visual interest. The bugle trim on the pillow (left) and the dark fringe on the red-and-white-stripe silk curtains (right) are charming refinements on otherwise plain fabrics.**

OPPOSITE, BOTTOM LEFT **Here, green polka-dot trim is used to create a picture frame in the center of this white pillow, and the polka-dot fabric is used again to bind the edges of the pillow.**

OPPOSITE, BOTTOM RIGHT **Use accessories to bring interesting color contrasts into a room, like this rich red pillow with button trims and decorative welting against the beige couch with appliquéd flowers in red.**

ABOVE **Include photos of rooms in your Look Book that combine items and materials of different textures and finishes, because variety in your decor will make it much more interesting. My house is filled with items of several materials, as you can see in my kitchen, where I used tile, granite, and metal.**

OPPOSITE **My husband, who works with me in my design business, built this buffet for me many years ago, and we recently decided to update it (it had too much sentimental value to get rid of it). I cut down the original doors, replaced the hardware, and used picture-frame molding and Formica for the doors and horn spoons from Africa for the door pulls.**

In addition, research shopping allows you to make a dimensional study of furniture and space. In other words, it gives you an opportunity to see, touch, and try out potential purchases. After all, what looks good in a magazine or a brochure may not look quite like you imagined in reality.

When you're out doing research, it's a good idea to bring a small camera with you. As you come across something that catches your eye, take a moment to snap a picture. Sometimes it's just a detail that you're interested in. Make certain to include your notes on the back of the photograph or in your notebook. But if you use a notebook, don't forget to transfer your notes onto the back of the photo later.

The photos from your research shopping don't need to include measurements for art, accessories, and lamps, but they should try to include some notations on size for furniture. Oftentimes you can ask for some promotional material—a brochure or flyer—on the items you are interested in. If these are not available, a photo will suffice. Since some companies offer different fabric selections for seating (sofas and chairs), it would be a good idea to photograph your fabric selection or obtain a sample for your Look Book. Just ask your salesperson; you might be surprised how helpful they can be. A friend of mine was actually told once that she could take an ottoman home to preview the fabric! But of course, you will be sure to encounter aggressive salespeople, too. Don't allow yourself to be pressured into a purchase before you are ready. I know it's hard, but open up your Look Book, hold it close to your face, and use it as a shield until you are out of danger!

And by all means, don't limit the photos in your Look Book to items you have yet to purchase; include photographs of the treasures you already own. Just be sure they are really treasures. In my career, I've met many people who have paid hundreds of dollars to move or store something only to realize that it either didn't work in their new home or that they took it because it was given to them and not necessarily because they liked it. If you use one of these "treasures" in your newly designed space, it can potentially ruin a great look.

Organize Your Look Book

NOW THAT YOU HAVE GATHERED your inspiration photos from magazines and lots of photos and brochures from research shopping trips, it's time to organize all of this to create a book that will make shopping and decision-making much easier. You will need a three-ring binder, divider tabs, and clear sheet protectors.

1 **FLOOR PLAN** Your floor plan should be located on page 1, complete with measurements and indications of the location of mechanical and structural items.

2 **CREATE SECTIONS FOR EACH ROOM** Use the divider tabs to create sections for every room you are designing. If you are only designing one room, divide the book into categories, such as furnishings, accessories, and fabrics.

3 **FILE YOUR PHOTOS** Place each photo in a sheet protector and file them in the appropriate section. If you're planning to use the same item in multiple rooms, make certain to include copies in each section.

4 **REVIEW AND EDIT** Once you've organized your photos, review your book carefully. You'll probably notice that many of your selections have a similar look. This is good, because it means that you know what you like. On the other hand, if you discover during this review that your selections are radically different, you need to take the time to reevaluate them. While there is nothing wrong with diversity, too much will hamper your efforts to achieve a harmonious interior.

Your Look Book is finally done, the result of hours of research. Full of photographs and clippings, it represents both a guide to your design and a wish list. Be proud of your accomplishment: it takes a lot of dedication to reach this point!

There may be some of you who question the value of a Look Book by arguing that the designs it features were created with someone else in mind and that the design conception you will create

This was the first award-winning interior of my career. It's important to note that part of the reason the award was bestowed was because the design was created on a limited budget. This proves that great interior design doesn't have to be prohibitively expensive.

using these photos as a guide will not be original, but rather recycled from other designers' ideas. And to that I would respond: "So what?" Consider this collection of photos as you would a coloring book or a paint-by-numbers canvas. While it is true a professional artist created the images, your hands changed the colors, filled in the blanks, and gave them definition. Not to mention that much time and thought went into the professional designs featured in magazines, so why shouldn't you use them to your advantage?

Others may be concerned that the rooms featured in magazines are often prepared with unlimited budgets. Since most people have budgets they must stay within, they question the practicality of basing a design scheme on something so clearly out of their price range. As with clothing, it is possible to find furniture "fashions" of similar styles with prices that range from high to low. It may take a little longer, but it is certainly possible. Style is not about spending a lot of money. But if this concerns you, and your budget allows, you can mix one or two more expensive items into your design along with more budget-friendly items. It adds a layer of richness to your interior, but won't break the bank.

While I've reached a period in my career where all of my jobs have virtually unlimited budgets, there was a time when that was not the case. Taking a limited budget and turning it into a beautiful and functional interior is what launched my success. In fact, I received an interior design award from the International Decorator's Guild (IDG) and much public praise for my creative use of limited space and a limited budget on one particular project (see a photo of it opposite).

And just between you and me, I've seen many houses decorated with unlimited budgets that have been unbelievably ugly as a result of lack of design knowledge. So, take heart—with the right information, a beautiful interior is possible for everyone regardless of budget.

STEP

2

Let's Review

Creating a Look Book is an essential part of preparing to design your home. By collecting photos from magazines of rooms that you would like to inspire your home decor, you begin to get a much more focused idea of your likes and dislikes. These photos, as well as the photos and brochures from research shopping trips, will make decisions about your final purchases much easier.

When perusing the magazines, select photos of rooms that appeal to your taste and work with your lifestyle. Choose rooms that are the same size as the ones you are decorating. Keep the following things in mind as you compile your photos:

1 After you have chosen an inspiration room photo, analyze every aspect of the room, especially featured items, such as color, fabrics, furniture size and arrangement, and art.

2 Include photos of detail and specialty items that appeal to you, and keep pictures and notes of the items you find on your research shopping trips. Don't forget to include swatches of fabric, samples of wallpaper, as well as photos of items you already own that you want to incorporate into your decor.

3 Use a three-ring binder and sheet protectors to organize your photos. Your floor plan should begin the book on page 1, and sections should correspond to the rooms you are going to design. If you are working on one room, divide your notebook into categories, such as furnishings, accessories, and fabrics.

4 Keep it with you while shopping and update as necessary.

Create a Furniture Plan

I try not to be "on the job" when I haven't been hired, but sometimes it's so hard to do. There have been many times when I have been in a house in which the furniture layout didn't look balanced. I've seen coffee tables located so far from the sofa and chairs, they seemed to be on display rather than a vital part of the furniture grouping. I've been in rooms with so many furnishings, I felt I had to turn sideways to move around, and I've even seen walls so crowded with accessories and art that you could barely see the wall they were on. Mistakes like these will have a negative effect not only on your impression of how a room looks, but more importantly how the room functions. At the end of the design process, you will have spent countless hours making decisions about your flooring, the style and color of your furnishings, as well as art and accessories, but if you neglect function, all of your work will be for naught.

I believe there are probably a number of reasons why people create plans that don't suit their needs or work with the specific details of their space, but I think mainly it is because they don't understand that interior design is a combination of art and science. The "art" aspect relates to achieving a pleasing balance of furnishings and accessories in a space. The "science" aspect relates to creating a design that accommodates how the body moves and functions. Both categories play important roles in the creation of a successful interior design. Before you can understand how to place furniture for decorative purposes, however, you have to first understand the science of interior design.

OPPOSITE **In dining rooms, allowing enough room between those seated at the table is a necessity if you want to eat comfortably.**

The Human Body and Its Relation to Space

WHEN DESIGNING A ROOM, you must know how much space the body needs to walk, bend, reach, sit, etc. I know this seems obvious, but you would be surprised how many people don't account for this when designing their space. There are generally accepted measurements and formulas to allow each of these functions and I share them below. (It's important to note that all of these measurements are based on the average body size.)

For a room to be truly enjoyable and inviting, it not only needs furnishings made of fabrics and materials you love to lounge on, there needs to be ample space for you and your guests to walk around easily.

BODY SPACE FOR SEATING

Let's start with the body's relationship to sofas and coffee or cocktail tables. The coffee table should be a *maximum* of 18 inches in front of the sofa. There are three reasons for this:

1 **ARM REACH FROM SOFA TO TABLE** The average arm reach while seated is 18 inches. This distance will allow you to have a drink in your hand while seated on the sofa and be able to place the cup or glass on the table without sitting at the edge.
2 **WALK SPACE** The body needs 18 inches of space to walk between the sofa and the table. Leaving less than this is asking for an accident (or at least scuffed shins!).
3 **LEG SPACE** Legs need 18 inches to extend while seated. If there is less space than this, your guest may use your table base as a footrest!

End tables and night tables also need to be reachable, but they don't require walk space, so it's okay to place them against the seating. If you feel you need a little space, however, the maximum distance I recommend is 6 inches.

RIGHT **When seated on a sofa, the coffee table should be no more than 18 inches away from the sofa so that you can easily reach it without sitting on the edge. This also allows plenty of room for someone to walk between the sofa and the table.**

OPPOSITE **This detail of football star Ty Law's living room demonstrates the correct amount of space between a coffee table and a sofa. The serpentine curve of the sofa beautifully mirrors the glass-topped metal coffee table, which is actually a part from an airplane engine!**

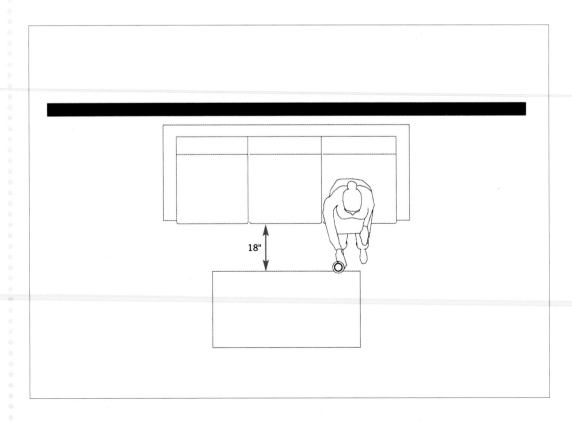

18"

ABOVE **Night tables in your bed-room should be close to the bed, and when accessorizing, leave enough room for small clocks, lamps, and telephones.**

RIGHT **Place end tables no more than 6 inches away from your sofa, and remember that they should never be deeper than your sofa.**

OPPOSITE **In my celebrity client's Florida hideaway, Egyptian-inspired carvings cover the chairs that flank a small round table in his living room, which is within easy reach to place glasses or other items.**

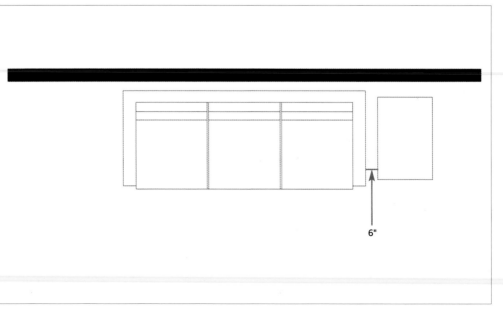

6"

BODY SPACE FOR CONVERSATION AREAS

In your home there are rooms (or at least one room) in which you'll arrange seating for conversation. This may be a living room, family room, study, or sitting room. Regardless of the rooms you choose, these areas will need to allow for conversations between two or more people. When planning the seating, the layout must be governed by speech and hearing patterns, so the maximum distance you should allow between people is 8 feet. This 8-foot distance is called the "conversation arc."

Seating areas in large rooms should adhere to the conversation arc as well. A large room has the advantage of accommodating two or more conversation groups. If you have a large room with one conversation area with space remaining and you don't want to use it for seating, use it as a music area (with a baby grand piano) or a game area (with a game table and chairs).

Like most of us, I love getting together with my family and friends and spending time at my home visiting. To make this as pleasant as possible, my furniture is arranged to allow everyone to be heard easily.

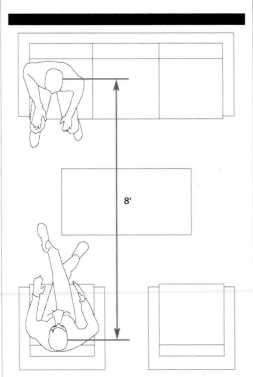

ABOVE The "conversation arc" is the ideal distance between speakers in a conversation grouping so everyone seated can hear each other well when talking. This distance should be 8 feet.

LEFT The furnishings in this living room are arranged according to the conversation arc.

BODY SPACE FOR BENDING AND KNEELING

If you find yourself bumping into walls whenever you bend down, don't head over to your local weight-loss meeting! It's probably just time to reassess how much space you have allowed for bending and kneeling.

There are two rooms that require a lot of bending and kneeling: the kitchen, where we bend to put away dishes and pots, to clean, and to unload the dishwasher; and in the bedroom, where we bend to open dresser drawers and make beds. Bending may also be necessary in other rooms where you need to remove items from lower cabinets. In all of these cases, 3 feet or more of bending space is required between the furniture and the wall or from one piece of furniture to another. When determining your furniture arrangements in any of these rooms, be sure to give yourself adequate space to perform daily chores.

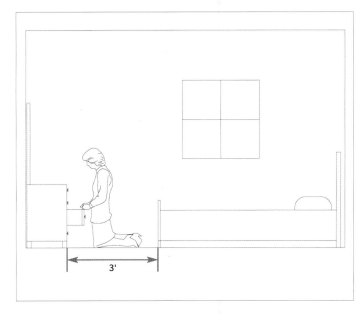

ABOVE **Always leave sufficient space between furnishings to allow for bending and kneeling— I suggest at least 3 feet.**

LEFT **In working rooms, such as kitchens, easy access and functionality are very important, so make sure you have enough room to bend to reach items in lower cabinets.**

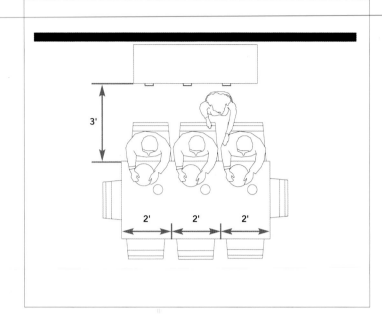

BODY SPACE FOR DINING

The number of people you want to comfortably seat determines your dining table size, and the room size determines the table size. When seated at the table, the body needs 2 feet of space per person to allow adequate elbowroom when dining. This doesn't mean that the width of the dining chair should be 2 feet (in fact, it may often be less), but that you should allocate 2 feet per person of table space.

But there is more to dining than eating. Dining involves eating *and* talking, both during and after the meal, so there should be space around the dining table, what I call "push back and walk" space. You need at least 3 feet of free space on all sides of the table, because most diners tend to push away from the table to talk, while the host or caterer walks behind them to clear the table. The diagram at left will give you a better idea of the necessary space for dining.

ABOVE **For a more pleasurable dining experience, allow 2 feet of table space per person in a dining room and 3 feet of space between the table and other furniture in the room, such as a buffet.**

RIGHT **I used beautiful Japanese ash wood for the table, chairs, built-in buffet, and carpentry in this dining room. Because the room is so large, I chose to turn the dining table on an angle for added emphasis, but this still allowed the necessary space around the table.**

OPPOSITE **The buffet in my celebrity client's dining room was constructed using an interesting combination of horn laminate and limestone for the top. The natural grass cloth for the wallcovering and wood furnishings keep the room warm and welcoming.**

The body requirements and measurements needed to make your interior functional and comfortable have already been taken into consideration by architects and furniture designers. These professionals design their products with the function and size of the body in mind. It's up to you, however, to determine whether the placement of your furnishings within the space also takes these essential concerns into account.

I realize that some of you may have trouble with feeling confident about furniture arranging. And because sofas, wall units, and other heavy furniture are not so easy to move around to experiment with different arrangements, I have created Cecil's Get It Right! Furniture Patterns to assist you in space planning (see Sources on page 174 for information on how to order). These are lifesize paper patterns that you lay on the floor to try out arrangements quickly and easily. The patterns come in standard furniture sizes, but can be customized to match the size and shape of your furniture exactly. By using the patterns, you will be able to view your proposed furniture layout. When you are done, actually walk through it and see if there are any potential problems.

Decorative Items and Space

A FURNITURE ARRANGEMENT that you can navigate around easily is important, but the furnishings and accessories must also look good as an ensemble—that is, they must be balanced in relation to each other and in relation to the space they occupy. To do this, you must understand how to create the proper proportions.

BALANCING FURNITURE AND WALLS
Generally—the dining room excluded—large furniture items are placed in front of a wall.

The relationship of the wall to the sofa is determined by the size of your sofa, because most likely you can't change the size of your wall, but you can select a sofa size that balances it. Your sofa should be between half to three-quarters the length of the wall. If it's less, it will seem like the proportions are wrong. Just remember to leave at least 18 inches of wall space on either side of the sofa for end tables or accessories.

LEFT **This handsome entertainment unit made of red oak with a cherry stain is a focal point of the room because of its size and beautiful, warm color.**

OPPOSITE **In my living room, a 15-foot sofa is placed against the 20-foot-long wall. To balance the room properly, I created a coffee table that is about two-thirds the size of the sofa.**

To create balance between a bed and the wall it's against, what is important is how much of the wall the bed covers. Since the bed is the natural focal point of any bedroom, the size of the bed will depend on the wall where you want to place it. You should always plan to leave at least 3 feet of unused space on either side of the bed. For example, let's say you have a king-size bed and the mattress is 6 feet wide. When you add 3 feet of space on the right and the left, the arrangement needs a 12-foot wall.

Wall units—such as entertainment units, library bookshelves, and display cabinets—can be so large they actually seem to become the wall.

Entertainment units that house television and audio equipment balance a room best when they cover 80–100 percent of the wall. Because of their size, they become a focal point and can make a wonderful design statement. I have discovered that the continuous lines of a large entertainment unit (or one that covers the entire wall) make a room appear larger than it is. Consoles, buffets, breakfronts, armoires, and étagères can be as small as half the length of the wall, because they are generally accompanied by chairs, mirrors, paintings, sconces, art, and accessories.

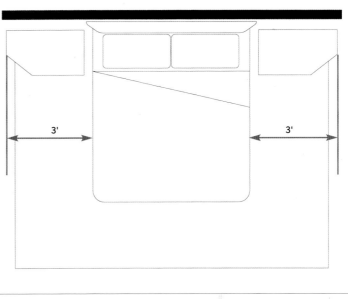

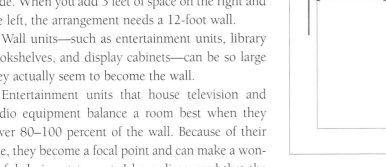

ABOVE **Allow 3 feet of space around your bed to move around it easily.**

OPPOSITE **In this majestic bedroom with a high ceiling, I installed fiber optic lighting to resemble stars. I was careful to leave ample room around the bed.**

LEFT **I used white oak for the wall unit in this spacious living room. Because wall units tend to cover a large majority of a wall, like this one, I used a light-colored wood so that the effect would not feel too overpowering.**

ABOVE **My clients use this family room primarily for entertaining. The large wall unit houses the TV, as well as their extensive collection of artifacts from around the world. In spite of the fact that it is a large room, I made sure that the furniture arrangement adhered to the principle of the conversation arc so that regardless of where you sat, it was easy to hear people talk across the room.**

OPPOSITE **I designed and built this wall unit and wet bar using a variety of materials, including wood, metal and tile accents, glass doors, and granite counters.**

RIGHT **Chairs in conversation groupings, like the French upholstered chairs in this elegant living room, should be between one-quarter and one-half the size of the sofa.**

BELOW RIGHT **Another view of the room at right showing the ottoman on the other side of the coffee table. Ottomans and other backless seating are a great addition to any room.**

BELOW **I paired this French-country console table with a blue chenille sofa. A console table should never be taller than the sofa.**

BALANCING FURNITURE

The best way to determine the appropriate size of a coffee table for your room is to select the sofa keeping in mind the sofa-to-wall proportion discussed above. The coffee table in your room should be approximately two-thirds the size of the sofa. If you have a coffee table already and it is not two-thirds the size of your sofa, consider changing it.

Accent tables and end tables are very important to conversation groupings. Your selection should be based on what fits at the end of or between the seating. Never select an end table that is deeper than the seating it is adjacent to.

Console or sofa tables are generally placed directly behind the sofa. For the best results, the sofa and console should be about the same length. A console should *never* be longer than the sofa. Additionally, the console should be the same height or a little shorter than the sofa back.

Chairs are generally located in the middle of the floor space rather than against the walls. Not only must the arrangement of chairs and other seating adhere to the principle of the conversation arc, but the chairs must also balance the room and the sofa. Allow the largest item in the grouping—generally the sofa—to help you determine what size chairs you should use. Choose chairs as large as half the size or as small as one-quarter the size of the sofa length. One exception to this rule is if you have a large modular sofa, such as an L-shaped sofa.

Benches or ottomans are nice additions to conversation groupings. When an area in a room seems a bit empty, but the space size is too small for a chair or sofa, they may be the perfect solution.

STEP

3

Let's Review

To create a furniture plan that is functional and looks good, you need to know how the body moves in a space as well as the proper proportions for furniture in relation to each other and the space they are in.

To ensure you move around the furniture in a room easily, keep the following in mind:
- A coffee table should be no more than 18 inches from the sofa so that you can easily reach items on it, and end tables should be no more than 6 inches from the sofa.
- In rooms where you have conversation groupings, people should not be more than 8 feet apart.
- For any room where bending or kneeling is required, allow 3 feet of space between furnishings and walls.
- In the dining room there should be 3 feet between the table and other furniture, such as a china cabinet, or the wall.
- The dining room table should allow for 2 feet of table space per person.

To ensure that the proportions of the furniture in your room are correct, keep the following in mind:
- The sofa should be between half to three-quarters the length of the wall it is placed against.
- Always allow 3 feet of space on either side of the bed.
- Wall units should cover 80–100 percent of a wall.
- The coffee table should be approximately two-thirds the size of the sofa.
- Consoles and buffets, when used against a wall, may be as small as half the size of the wall.
- Chairs can be between one-quarter and half the size of the sofa.
- Console tables should not be longer than the sofa they are placed against, nor should they be higher than the sofa back.
- End tables should never be deeper than the sofa they are adjacent to.

Decorate One Layer at a Time

Before we go any further, I need to remind you that in interior design, each step builds on the one before. So you need to read the previous steps and complete your "homework" before you proceed with Step 4. You won't achieve satisfactory results if you've skipped the preliminary steps.

Step 4 offers more detailed information on selecting decorative items. But in this chapter, I am not concerned with the size and scale of the decorative items in a space, but rather the total number of items you have in a room. In order to know the proper distribution of decorative items, I have devised what I call a "ratio recipe."

Much like a recipe you follow to bake a cake, for example, my ratio recipe indicates what percentage of the total items in a room will be distributed in the three areas, or layers, of a room—the floor, walls, and ceiling. Following this recipe will make many of the decisions about which items to purchase for your room much easier. Decorative items in a room should be distributed in this ratio: 65 percent of the items will be on the floor; 25 percent of the items will be on the walls; and 10 percent of the items will be on the ceiling.

I determined this ratio recipe early in my career. Some of my clients were first-time buyers of custom homes, and it was not uncommon for them to get carried away with upgrading items such as door hardware, flooring, and plumbing fixtures. As a result, the budget for furniture was so drastically reduced they only had enough to furnish one room. The moral of the story: if you're on a budget, keep in mind all the layers as you shop.

OPPOSITE **To create this sophisticated kitchen, I used black granite floor tiles, a stainless steel cook-top island, and stainless steel bar stools with tan leather upholstery for layer one—the floor. For layer two—the walls—I installed silver metallic wallpaper, then added stainless steel and smoked glass cabinetry, black granite countertops and back splash, stainless steel appliances, and a black double wall oven. Layer three—the ceiling—was decorated with recessed high-hat lighting.**

Furniture Styles: Something for Everyone

THERE ARE SO MANY STYLES to choose from: contemporary, art deco, Victorian, modern, traditional—the list goes on and on. You probably already know what appeals to you, however, according to industry studies, most people choose traditional or transitional furnishings for their home. In fact, an impressive 75–85 percent of all furniture purchases are in the traditional style.

Many people don't understand the difference between traditional and transitional style. Transitional is a simplified version of traditional. For example, consider a Louis XV traditional chair: the transitional version would be more streamlined, with fewer ornate carvings and details, and sleeker arms and legs.

Modern furniture is inspired by styles of the early to mid-twentieth century, when clean lines and industrial materials were replacing the overly decorative styles of the late nineteenth century. Materials frequently used for modern furnishings are Italian leather, molded polyurethane, stainless steel, and glass.

This room illustrates my "ratio recipe" perfectly: the majority of the decorative items are located on the floor with some items on the wall (such as the faux finish with a silver metallic paint), and just a few items are on the ceiling.

Urban and Asian minimalism have become very popular lately, and both styles tend to use lots of dark neutrals. While some feel that these styles can be too severe or stark, many like the simplicity and uncluttered feel of a space filled with this style of furnishings.

Another popular style now is Moroccan inspired. While most of what is available is art and accessories, furniture is becoming more widely available. If the exotic feel and rich colors associated with it appeals to you, I recommend you only use a few accessories or small pieces of furniture—like an accent table—because if you base your entire interior design on this style, it may feel dated before too long.

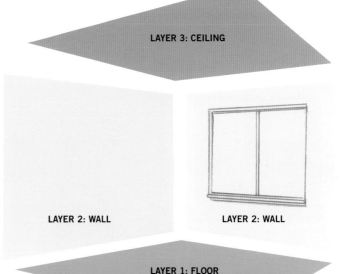

This diagram illustrates my system of dividing a room into three decorative layers: the floor, the walls, and the ceiling.

Layer One: Floor

THE MAJORITY OF DECORATIVE ITEMS in a room—65 percent—will be on the floor. Seating will comprise most of the items on the floor. Tables of all types are the second largest group of decorative items in this layer. Consoles, buffets, and display and other storage units are the third group.

SEATING

Seating is very important in a room, so it's advisable to make decisions about these furnishings first, and there are many types to choose from. Of course, the sofa is a must-have, and most styles are available with matching armchairs and tufted ottomans. A recent trend is to combine a sofa with a chaise lounge for the ultimate experience in comfort. The chaise lounge is generally associated with formal period interiors, but they are now widely available in contemporary styles.

Sleeper sofas today are very different from the cumbersome and uncomfortable sleepers we remember from years ago. Lighter and more stylish, these updated sofas are still a convenient and space-saving necessity for those who don't have a guest bedroom. A new incarnation of the traditional sleeper is the versatile pullout lounger/sleeper, which functions similarly to the classic futon. There is no separate mattress; instead, the sofa transforms itself into a bed. Pull on the front, and it becomes a lounger, and if you pull a little more, the lounger becomes a full-length reclining bed. And if you pull just a bit more, it becomes a flat bed.

The modular seating we associate with the 1970s is still available, but it is much smaller and lighter. It's a great choice for a room, because it allows some flexibility in your design, but provides lots of seating. Because of the advantages this type of seating offers, furniture manufacturers now make it for the outdoors.

Depending on the size of your space, most people opt to have at least one chair in a conversation grouping. Side chairs are enjoying a new popularity, as is the club chair. But, of course, old habits are hard to break, and the recliner remains an old favorite. It's been updated, though, and the new designs will suit a wide range of tastes.

As mentioned in Step 2, furniture is manufactured in standard sizes, and I have included these standard sizes for the most common furniture items in the Appendix on page 172. Knowing these sizes will help considerably as you design your room, making it possible to plan the furniture arrangement *before* selecting the final pieces.

I've been designing and manufacturing furniture for my clients for many years. In that time, I've never had a client question the proportion and scale of my designs for wall units and tables. There have been, however, a few questions and concerns about the comfort of my custom seating—concerns which, I am pleased to say, always seem to disappear when my clients sit on the finished piece.

The decor in the master bedroom is an example of the "peaceful coexistence" approach to decorating windows and walls (explained later in this chapter): both are covered in a soft beige moiré silk, so there is only a subtle difference between them.

Furniture design may not be rocket science, but it is still a science. The key to creating a comfortable custom design is to use the standard inside measurements, including standard seat height and the pitch of the back. These measurements are all based on the anatomy of the average body size. Of course, if you are not an average-size person, these measurements will need to be reexamined.

I have designed homes for many athletes, and in particular NBA players, such as P. J. Brown. Like many basketball players, he is over 7 feet tall, and even his wife is tall—just over 6 feet. That's quite a difference from the height of the average consumer of 5 feet 8 inches! It was clear that I would need to design custom furniture for them. On paper, my custom sofa (which was 4 feet deep, more than 1 foot deeper than the standard sofa) seemed right, but as it was being fabricated, I was worried. It looked enormous. But by the time it was ready to be delivered, it looked perfect, and when we installed it, I knew it would work. P. J. and Dee arrived soon after and sat down. As soon as he did, P. J., with a wide grin and looking relaxed, said, "Now this is what I am talking about!" What a difference the right measurements can make in creating comfortable seating.

TABLES

The table—coffee, end, accent, and dining—comes in a huge variety of styles and materials, though most people prefer wood tables. Glass and acrylic tables are still a very popular option, but they show dirt easily, so those who want low-maintenance surfaces should opt for wood. For outdoor use, enameled bistro tables are currently making a comeback, and there is a big demand for natural, rot-resistant woods and outdoor wovens.

DISPLAY AND STORAGE UNITS

Most of us never feel we have enough display and storage furniture, such as consoles, buffets, and wall units. Of this type of furniture, wall units in particular come with a large variety of options: drawers, doors, open or closed shelving systems, or a combination of all of the above. These kinds of furnishings have undergone significant design changes lately, due mostly to the changing size of TVs, stereos, and other audio-visual equipment. Electronics are now larger and thinner, so the need for deep wall units is not as great as it once was. Nevertheless, the larger units allow for much-needed storage space for other items.

Layer Two: Walls

WALLS ARE THE SECOND decorative layer in a room. While only 25 percent of the items in a room (including windows and doors) will be on the walls, it can seem like those elements have a greater impact on the finished decor than those on the floor, even though there are fewer of them. There are several reasons for this: walls occupy the most square footage in any room, and because they are vertical and surround you, you are always aware of them. In a balanced decor, wall decoration will bring the overall composition together.

The medium green paint in this bedroom pairs beautifully with wood and neutral tones of the furnishings and accessories.

Unlike decorative items for the floor, decorative items for the walls do not need to address body function, which offers you more choice in your selections. Although I caution you not to overdecorate your walls, this is an area where you can be creative. In my work, I routinely try combinations of items on the wall that I wouldn't dare try on the floor. The fun part is that you can pair flat items with three-dimensional items and mix textured wallcoverings with smooth ones for a unique look. And because your wall decor is entirely up to you—unlike furniture where the design is determined by the manufacturer—you can decorate them to reflect your personal taste and style.

WALLCOVERINGS

There are six basic wallcoverings:

1 Paint
2 Wallpaper
3 Faux finishes, murals, and trompe l'oeil
4 Wood paneling
5 Mirrors
6 Decorative wall molding

Paint is the perfect wallcovering for any budget. Light yellow can make a room feel airy and fresh, and in this example it makes the reds in the bedding and art more brilliant (above); and the pink walls create a lively background for the predominantly white furniture in this dining room (right).

Paint

I discovered the creative potential of paint long before I became an interior designer. My first career was as an art teacher in the public school system of a small town in Georgia, a town so small it had no apartment complexes. The second year I taught there, I rented a space that had once provided housing for migrant farm workers. It was a mess. Most people would have taken one look at that space and would have run straight out and never looked back. But for me it was better than renting a room in someone's house.

My challenge was to make this small space habitable. A thorough cleaning made a huge difference, and adding my creative touch made it even better. These were not expensive changes, because I was working with an extremely limited—well, nonexistent!—budget, but it became a comfortable space, nonetheless. By making a few improvements—and painting was key among them—I created a welcoming home for myself, not just a place to live. The experience also taught me a valuable lesson about how uplifting decorating your home can be.

Paint is the most popular wallcovering for several reasons: it is relatively inexpensive, you can apply it yourself, and it's easy to change if you don't like the finished result.

Paint is the ideal material to bring color into a decor. Bold color choices create lively interior designs, like in this bathroom, in which the walls are painted in a striking combination of light purple and grass green.

Before you choose a color for your walls, there are a few things you should keep in mind regarding how color will affect the overall impression of your room. (Color will be discussed in more depth in Step 6, beginning on page 111.)

- White or light colors (which are comprised of 75 percent white) are perfect for a room that contains fabrics of many colors and patterns. Art collectors may also want to consider a color scheme that relies heavily on white or light colors, since art is best showcased against these colors.

- Bright or intense colors (such as red, green, yellow, and blue) should be used when you want to create a dramatic effect or a feeling of warmth. Many times bright colors make a room appear smaller, but the impact of the look will often offset the impression of decreased size. If you want to use an intense color, but you don't want your room to appear smaller, use the color on one accent wall. Choose the wall that faces you when you enter the room or the wall that has the main composition of furnishings against it (such as the sofa wall).

- Dark colors, such as black, dark gray, or brown, can create a more formal, subdued look. These colors are particularly popular in "hi-tech" or contemporary interiors, because the dark colors work well with the reflective materials such as stainless steel, chrome, glass, and mirror that these interiors generally feature.

USE THIS COLOR . . .

SW 6852
Desire Pink

SW 6853
Fussy Pink

IF YOU LIKE THIS COLOR.

Choosing the correct color paint for your walls can be tricky, because the translation from the small paint swatch to the large expanse of the wall can make the color seem too dark. I suggest choosing your color and stepping down two shades to achieve the desired result. For example, using the paint swatch above, if you like the third color from the top, choose the first one on the swatch, which is two shades lighter.

Cecil Says

Be aware that when selecting your paint color from a small sample, the color will appear much more intense when used on the wall. To avoid ending up with a color that is not what you intended, I recommend that you identify the color you like on the paint swatch, and then choose a color two to three shades lighter for the final color. This is more likely the color you want for the finished wall.

Wallpaper

Wallpaper comes in a dizzying variety of colors and materials, including metal and plastic, so it suits a wide range of tastes. While it is more involved than painting, it doesn't necessarily need to be installed by a professional. Mistakes, however, are more costly and correction more labor intensive, so care should be taken when selecting and installing it.

Why use wallpaper? Some of the advantages are:

- Adds pattern to walls
- Gives dimension to walls
- Creates texture
- Is available with matching upholstery fabric
- Fixes acoustical issues by providing sound control
- Is available in easily maintainable surfaces (i.e., washable)

YOUR GOAL: ADD PATTERN

Here are some helpful hints when selecting wallpaper to add pattern to your walls:

- Patterns on a wall are like patterns on a dress: just as the kind of patterned dress you wear will depend on your body type, patterned wallpaper must work with the shape and size of the room.

- A vertical stripe pattern is good for rooms with low ceilings, because the lines add height. Rooms that are small or average-size work best with subtle tone-on-tone (two shades of the same color) stripes.

- Wallpaper with small patterns such as flowers or geometrical shapes is a great selection when using other wall decoration.

ABOVE **This entrance foyer has a low 7-foot ceiling, but I used wallpaper with narrow, vertical stripes to create an impression of height.**

LEFT **I used a silk fabric with subtle stripes of pink, yellow, green, and purple to add pattern and a slight texture to the walls.**

- Large, bold-patterned wallpaper should be used in large rooms. It can, however, look good in average-size rooms on an accent wall. The accent wall must be the one with the large furniture (such as the bed wall) or opposite the wall with large furniture so that the room feels more balanced. Bold wallpaper in a room without large furnishings may need to be balanced by using oversize framed mirrors or understated consoles.

- There is one small room where it is acceptable to use bold wallpaper—the powder room.

YOUR GOAL: CREATE DIMENSION

Wallpaper that has a texture or a relief—or has been painted to appear textured—can be used to give dimension to the walls. These types of wallpaper can offer a variety of effects: they can add much needed architectural detailing to an otherwise plain room, or they can create warmth by using natural fibers, such as grass cloth.

The true purpose of this type of wallpaper is to add visual interest and tactility to flat surfaces. Most of these wallpapers do not have a printed pattern, which allows them to be used in any room regardless of its size.

RIGHT **Wallpaper with a small pattern was used on the walls in this sitting room. The matching upholstery creates a nice continuity with the wallcovering.**

OPPOSITE **Accent walls using wallpaper can be a very attractive feature of a room. In this bedroom, the bold-patterned wallpaper would have been too overwhelming on every wall, so it was used only on the bed wall. The pattern is used for the bedspread, and the throw pillows have a smaller version of the same pattern. Striped pillow shams and window treatments pick up colors from the floral patterns.**

Specialty wallpapers are widely available now and can create a very unique look. In this powder room, what looks like mirrored tile is actually foil wallpaper. The slight reflective quality of the paper provides the perfect background for the ornate Venetian mirror and crystal vessel sink.

YOUR GOAL: MATCH WALLPAPER AND FABRIC

Many people like to be able to match their wallpaper and upholstery fabrics. If you do this in your interior, be sure not to place the furniture item immediately next to the wall as the repetition will be overwhelming. Keeping the eye moving over the various items in a room is one of the goals of interior design and one of the ways to ensure you do this is not to place items with the same pattern adjacent to each other.

YOUR GOAL: RECTIFY ACOUSTICAL ISSUES

Acoustical wallpaper provides sound control. I know from personal experience that open-style homes, with their high ceilings, often have an echo problem. My own home is an open space from the foyer through the dining, living, and family rooms with 18-foot ceilings and hard surface flooring. To reduce the excess noise created by these features, I used a heavy, vinyl acoustical wallpaper to absorb much of the sound.

YOUR GOAL: DURABILITY

Plastic or vinyl wallpaper is popular because it is inexpensive, very durable, and is available in solid colors and patterns. It's an ideal choice for high-traffic areas or houses with small children.

We have all made mistakes when it comes to choosing a wallcovering. For example, I once selected a plain beige wallpaper for a client. After the installation, I was devastated to realize that it actually looked like semigloss paint. That would have been fine, except that the wallpaper cost twice as much as paint would have. So choose your wallcoverings with care, and if the wallpaper you've chosen looks like paint and feels like paint, then, by all means it should be paint.

Cecil Says

If you've had horrible experiences with wallpaper installations with obvious seams, you might want to consider vinyl wallpaper, which generally hangs seamlessly.

SPECIALTY WALLPAPER

For the person looking for more exotic or unusual wallpaper options, there are several varieties to choose from. Made of everything from thin metal to wood veneer, they are beautiful and are sure to make quite an impression on your guests. Be aware, however, that they are expensive and can be very fragile.

Faux Finishes, Murals, and Trompe l'oeil

Faux finishes, murals, and trompe l'oeil are artists' techniques, all of which are intended to trick the eye. The technique can be as simple as sponging two colors on the same wall or as detailed as a painted garden scene. In recent years, many people have been attracted to faux finishes because, unlike wallpaper, there are no seams, it doesn't come loose from the walls, and color and design are limited only by your imagination.

Faux finishes can be used on both smooth and textured walls. The technique has become so popular that home improvement stores, and even Sherwin-Williams paint stores, now offer free seminars on faux finishes. Some techniques that are more difficult, such as those involving Venetian plaster and marbleizing finishes, may require professional application.

For the past five years, faux finishes have been the wallcovering of choice among my clients. Many of these clients live in Florida, where humid weather exacerbates the problem of loose, visible wallpaper seams. People are opting to skip the hassle by using faux finishes in place of wallpaper.

Unlike simple faux finishes, murals and trompe l'oeil are best left to the professional artist. Reproductions of scenic vistas and vignettes painted directly on your wall by an artist replace framed paintings or other artwork. If you have decided you want a mural, it should be painted in realistic style. I strongly recommend creating murals or trompe l'oeil in a children's room or in any room that needs a view.

ABOVE **The simple lines of the furnishings in this room contrast nicely with the mottled effect of the deep green faux finish.**

LEFT **Faux finishes are appropriate for any room in a house. There are dozens of techniques to create these finishes, many of which can be applied by the novice decorator.**

Wood paneling and molding are ideal choices for offices, studies, and libraries. The custom cherry-wood paneling used here is complemented by matching wood mini-blinds.

Wood Paneling

Wood paneling has come a long way since the 1960s, when it was used as a substitute for drywall or an inexpensive way to cover existing brick or cinderblock walls. Unfortunately, most of us remember that it looked inexpensive, too! Today, however, wood paneling can look sophisticated and elegant. It works well in both traditional or contemporary interiors, as well as in a range of other styles. And it can still be used to cover walls that are unappealing for whatever reason.

Mirrors can enlarge a space considerably, like in this bedroom where a wall of mirror was installed behind the bed.

BELOW **Wallcoverings aren't limited to paint, wallpaper, or molding. My clients wanted something unusual in the powder room of their Florida home, so we used coral stone on the walls to create a very unexpected and out-of-the-ordinary decor.**

Mirrors

Mirrors used as wallcoverings have two purposes: to reflect a view or another pleasing image from a different part of the room and to enlarge a space. Before you install a wall of mirror, however, careful consideration should be given to which wall to cover, because you want to be sure that what is reflected in the mirror is exactly what you want to look at.

Mirrored walls work well in bedrooms, bathrooms, dressing rooms, and exercise rooms. For those of you who believe that if something is good, more of it is better, I caution you that this does not apply to this application, because the image in the mirror will repeat. For example, two mirrored walls in a dining room can make 10 dining room chairs seem like 20, creating a sense that the room is crowded. However, I don't recommend using mirrored walls in the dining room (do you really want to see yourself and your guests chewing?) or the toilet areas in the bathroom (for obvious reasons).

Decorative Wall Molding

If there is one great wallcovering that is perfect for emphasizing architectural features, it's wall molding. Best used to divide a wall surface, molding adds beautiful detail to a wall, and brings an element of design to a long, plain wall.

Decorative moldings can be used with any or all of the wallcoverings we have already mentioned. It is extremely versatile and works well with a variety of styles. Wall molding in a traditional room should have a profile (or contour when viewed from the side). A contemporary room can feature either profile or flat molding.

Mirrors or wallpaper applied to a portion of a wall can be framed with wall molding. In fact, using molding around mirrors in this manner creates a very sophisticated look.

Molding that divides a wall is called "chair rail." Installation of chair rail allows two different wallcoverings to work together on the same wall. For example, you can paint the top half above the chair rail and apply a faux finish or wallpaper on the bottom half.

When selecting molding, you can use builder's material—which is generally used around doors and windows—and paint, stain, or apply a faux finish to it for an elegant look. Or you can use picture molding, which is used for framing art or mirrors. This type of molding comes in all shapes and sizes and is often intricately carved. One advantage of picture molding is that it is less expensive than carved decorative molding.

The trick to successfully using wall molding is knowing the right proportion in relation to the ceiling height and room size. I suggest 2-inch- to 3-inch-wide molding in the average-size room with a ceiling height of 8–10 feet. Using molding that is any smaller can make the application look cheap and will undermine your other efforts to create a beautiful room.

ABOVE **A combination of moldings in various sizes and styles has been applied to the walls in this room to add dimension to what was once a plain wall. The molding is used to dramatically emphasize two pieces of art.**

RIGHT **Chair rail molding can be used to create a separation between two types of wallcoverings on the same wall. In this instance, the molding divides the wall in half to delineate the different paint treatments.**

OPPOSITE **This French-country style dining room features molding as an integral part of the decor. Natural oak was used for the picture molding applied in boxes to the wall (which frames decorative plates and artwork).**

86

Dark green walls provide a contrasting backdrop for the green floral draperies in this room, which is a good example of the "opposites attract" approach to wallcoverings and window treatments.

WINDOWS AND WALLS

I am sure that many homeowners have found that their windows are located in places that don't suit them. And while it's true that the location and size of windows can create many obstacles to decorating, those windows—despite all evidence to the contrary—were not located in that precise place to make designing your house difficult. Architects generally determine the location of windows based on several considerations, including exterior balance, light exposure, and cross ventilation. They often select the size based on the need for emergency egress and/or because it is a standard size. These decisions often adversely impact the interior design, but the impact can be minimized, even counteracted. It's up to you to select window treatments that enhance and balance your room in spite of their location or size.

Let me give you an example of how I solved an extreme case of a poorly placed window.

When my niece and her husband purchased their first home, they brought with them an L-shaped sofa for their living room. The size of the sofa was perfect for the room, but the problem was that there was only one wall where they could place it and that wall had a window. The window was 4 feet above the floor and was about 4-feet square. The room already had excellent light exposure from two 6-foot sliding doors in an adjacent wall, so my solution was to hang a set of mini-blinds in the window (so it would look good from the outside), and then cover the opening with a large framed painting. While I certainly don't recommend this for most houses, it made sense in this case and proves that you can work with any situation!

WINDOW TREATMENTS

While this seems obvious, it bears repeating that windows are a part of the wall. Therefore, your wallcoverings and wall decor affect your windows and vice versa. You might want to think about it this way: windows and walls are married to each other, and there are two ways to describe this window-and-wall relationship: "opposites attract" and "peaceful coexistence."

Opposites Attract

In this approach, opulent wall treatments are paired with plain window treatments or the walls are plain and the window treatments are more dramatic by comparison. I consider walls to be "plain" if the coverings are: paint of any color, wallpaper that has a very faint pattern or design, a textured stucco finish in a solid color, wood panel with a subtle grain, or a faux finish with very little dimension or movement. (I don't use the word "plain" as a negative term. I simply mean that the walls are not overwhelmed with pattern or design.) With plain walls, window treatments can have more pattern or design, or some other feature, so they stand out.

There are many ways to create eye-catching window treatments. For inspiration, I have often looked at ladies' evening attire. Some gowns are sleek and simple; others are adorned with beads, tassels, and elaborate trims. Some are pleated, and others hang uninterrupted.

Drapery for window treatments, when inspired by evening dresses, can have a similar elegance and dramatic flair. You can use fabrics that have pattern on pattern, use tie-backs with a fringed edging, or even an embroidered organdy overskirt. And details like trims and tassels can make them even more attractive.

Opulent window treatments paired with a plain wall will be sure to make a room look amazing. The trick, however, is not to "overdress" your windows. You don't want to make the room feel like a fabric store!

Peaceful Coexistence

The other kind of approach to decorating windows and walls can be described as peaceful coexistence. In this approach, windows and walls have similar characteristics, and one doesn't outshine the other. For example, the walls can be a dark beige and the window treatments a light beige. They don't need to be covered in the same materials, but you want to create a harmonious pairing. This approach to walls and windows does not mean there is not a noticeable difference between the two, it just means there is a subtle difference.

The walls and window treatments in this bedroom are a good example of the "peaceful coexistence" approach. Both are in a very light color. The only bursts of intense color are in the throw blanket, throw pillows, and the chaise lounge.

In this master bedroom, the soft mocha color used for the draperies and wallcoverings creates a harmonious decor, which is punctuated with darker colors in the throw pillows, accessories, and door pulls in copper.

Here are a few more ideas. If your walls are covered in striped wallpaper, the window treatments would have a matching striped fabric. If your walls are covered in dark (or light) wood paneling, the window treatments would be dark (or light) wood shutters or blinds. Or, if the wallcovering is a fabric or wallpaper, you can take the same fabric or wallpaper and laminate it on verticals, window blinds, or roman shades.

How do you know which approach to follow? Here are a few suggestions.

WHEN TO USE THE "PEACEFUL COEXISTENCE" APPROACH

Employ this approach when you have one of the following scenarios:

- You want to make a small room look larger
- You don't like the location of the window
- You have a great light source, but a terrible view
- You don't want to detract from a gorgeous view

This treatment is usually simple with not too much fabric to cover the window, so it's an ideal option for a window that lets in a lot of light. If you use less fabric, this generally allows for greater light filtration. It's also a good option when you don't want to make the window a focal point, because the view is not very attractive.

WHEN TO USE THE "OPPOSITES ATTRACT" APPROACH

Employ this approach when you have one of the following scenarios:

- You have a very large room
- Your room has large picture windows
- You have a room with more glass surface than wall surface
- You wish to give prominence to a window

This approach works well in large rooms, because the more prominent treatments won't overwhelm the room. When you use a bolder pattern or color for a window treatment on a small window, this will help to offset the lack of balance created by the size of the window.

Using a bold pattern for the window treatments in this living room gave balance to the room by seeming to enlarge a small window.

If you have a view, you need to consider the size of the drapery stack when selecting a window treatment. The drapery stack is the amount of material gathered on the side or at the top of the window when the window treatments are fully opened. The size of your stack will depend on the type of material you've chosen, as well as the amount of material you have. I know from personal experience that the stack on either side can obscure a significant part of the view, and that is precisely what you don't want to do! This is more of a problem with fabric window treatments, but it can also affect other types of treatments as well.

Ask the person who is making up your window treatments how much space the material will take to stack, and then ask how much of it is going to be in the window. I have found that the worst window treatment for stacking is a roman shade. This doesn't mean that roman shades aren't beautiful treatments, but they may not be the option for someone who wants to avoid a large stack.

In many homes it isn't necessary to cover the windows. Certainly, if you feel that you don't want to cover them, then don't. Just keep in mind that there will be little privacy and that window treatments can help absorb sound in a space with lots of hard surfaces.

LEFT **A fabulous view without the need for privacy calls for a minimal window treatment. In this case, the cornice, with its nailhead trim, accents the window without covering the extraordinary view from this Colorado vacation home.**

OPPOSITE **When planning your window treatments, make certain you know how large the drapery stack will be, otherwise you may obscure your view.**

ADDING ART AND ACCESSORIES TO THE WALLS

Accessories, such as accent lighting (as opposed to task lighting) and art, add the finishing touches to wall decoration. Wall lights, or sconces, are very popular wall accessories. The tricky part, however, is that the location of the sconce must be determined long before the light fixture itself is ready to be installed. This is because wall lights require a junction box, which must be installed by an electrician. Junction boxes are typically located 6 feet above the floor, but you can customize this for your individual installation.

While it may seem like a relatively simple decision, determining where a junction box—and later a wall sconce—will be installed can have a lasting impact on the final decor. This is because the amount of space left around and between wall sconces will determine the size of the accessories or art that will be placed on the wall. In other words, if you want to hang a very large picture between two sconces, but don't take this into consideration when you have the junction boxes installed, you may find yourself having to rethink your original plan.

The placement of paintings and other wall art should be determined after installing the wallcoverings and creating a furniture arrangement. In my experience, the art has a way of letting you know where it wants to hang. Small art that is bright and colorful can work on large walls.

Not sure what art is best for your room? Use a framed mirror instead. To create a customized mirror, go to your local art framer and select a frame that you would use for a painting and use it for the mirror. The advantage is that you can get your frame in any size, color, or finish you want, and many times it will be less expensive than buying a ready-made framed mirror of comparable size.

I often think of a room's walls like a blank canvas that is just waiting for me to turn it into something attractive and interesting. I love to use accent lighting, which is available in a huge variety of styles and light quality. Decorative spotlights wash the walls in color (depending on the color of the bulb) or can be used to accent artwork.

Layer Three: Ceiling

THE THIRD DECORATIVE LAYER is the ceiling. Only 10 percent of the items in your room will be located there, and these items will be a combination of mechanical and decorative items. They include:

- Air conditioning and heater vents and fans
- Speakers and motion detectors
- Light fixtures and skylights
- Beams, soffits, and moldings
- Sprinklers

As you can see from this list, architects and engineers have already used much of the ceiling to meet the room's mechanical needs. This is very important to note: the items listed are just the items that you can see. There is actually much more that you can't see above the ceiling surface: wires, pipes, structural beams, air conditioning and heating ducts, and insulation, among other things. If you plan to add decorative items to the ceiling, like beams, soffits, and molding, it's vitally important to know the location of these mechanical items before you do anything. A nail or screw in the wrong location—like in the area of a water pipe or electrical conduit—can significantly dampen your enthusiasm for decorating!

Because ceilings are the smallest decorative layer, my advice is to keep it simple and put most of your budget toward items for the floor and walls. With that in mind, here are a few simple, low-cost options to enhance your ceilings.

PAINT

Ceilings painted in a light color give a room an airiness and make the ceiling seem higher than it is. Bright or dark colors in large rooms with high ceilings give a room character and work against the tendency of high ceilings to make furnishings seem small and out of scale. Trompe l'oeil or faux finishes applied to ceilings can actually make them "disappear." For example, an open-sky view painted on the ceiling can make you really feel that you are looking directly outside. I have used this technique in children's rooms and small areas, such as the area over bathtubs.

CROWN MOLDING

Another attractive option for giving a room dimension is crown molding, which can be used on both the ceiling and the wall. It's usually easy to install, since it is safe to nail molding to the top edge of the wall because very few mechanical items are found there.

> While most of us never really pay much attention to ceilings, they can actually have a significant impact on our impression of a room. In addition to lighting and other important features, the color of ceilings can make a room feel intimate and cozy or open and airy.

The light color used for the ceiling in this room helps distract you from its low height and prevents the room from feeling too small.

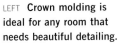

LEFT Crown molding is ideal for any room that needs beautiful detailing.

BELOW The ceiling in the loft area of this townhouse contains a skylight. The home-owner, however, wanted an intimate, exotic space for entertaining and watching television. To create this, yards of soft black fabric were draped between the exposed beams. This treatment radically alters the feel of the space, yet is easily removed should the homeowner desire a change at a future date.

Crown molding can be combined with wallcoverings such as paint and wallpaper very nicely. When using it with other wallcoverings, the ceiling is sectioned off with molding and then the sections are painted or wallpapered. This look can be very striking if the color of the paint and the molding are highly contrasted.

LIGHT FIXTURES

Ceiling-mounted light fixtures (including fans and track lighting) are another option to consider. These fixtures require a junction box, however, which must be installed by an electrician. It's important to note that some light fixtures, specifically those that hang from the ceiling, should not be considered part of the ceiling layer, because the eye sees it as part of the wall decor. When choosing one, such as a chandelier, keep in mind that it should coordinate with the wall decor.

OPPOSITE **While hanging fixtures are attached to the ceiling, I consider them part of the wall decor because they are viewed against the wall. Because of this, it's important that the style of your light fixture coordinates with your walls. Here the shape of the chandelier is similar to the table, and its brass trim mirrors the decorative band on the columns.**

STEP

4

Let's Review

Creating a balanced design is easy if you keep my ratio recipe in mind:
- **LAYER ONE: FLOOR** This layer should contain approximately 65 percent of the decorative items in the space.
- **LAYER TWO: WALLS** This layer should contain approximately 25 percent of the decorative items in the space, including windows and doors.
- **LAYER THREE: CEILING** This layer contains the final 10 percent of decorative items in the space.

The majority of decorative items in any room will be located on the floor, and most of those items will be seating. With the help of your Look Book and floor plan, shopping for items will be much easier.

Although only 25 percent of decorative items are located on the walls, these items can seem like the most prominent part of the decor. The reason for this is that the walls actually comprise the largest area of square footage in the room, and because they are always in your sight line, they have a greater impact on your impression of a room's design. I encourage you to try interesting combinations of wallcoverings, accessories, and art here, because these items don't have to be functional, so more creativity is allowed.

There are six basic types of wallcoverings:
- Paint
- Wallpaper
- Faux finishes, murals, and trompe l'oeil
- Wood paneling
- Mirrors
- Decorative wall molding

You won't add many items to the third decorative layer, the ceiling, as that area is generally reserved for mechanical items, such as air conditioning and heating vents. You can add visual interest to a ceiling by using a few inexpensive options: paint, light fixtures, or crown molding.

Mix Styles and Periods

Mixing decorative items of different styles and periods can create a very unique decor. For the nonprofessional, however, it can be overwhelming. But with a few tricks of the trade, you can do it effortlessly.

Several years ago I met a couple who hired me to design their Florida home. They wanted an open, contemporary design that featured wood and lots of different textures to add warmth and variety. They insisted that one item from their other house be incorporated into the design: a bowl that had been in the family for over 100 years. It was clear from my discussions with them that it had to be well showcased in the new house. We chose to display it on the dining room table. Not only did it work perfectly in the contemporary room, it was the focal point of the decor.

In this case, mixing items from different periods was simple. It didn't require a lot of thought as to how the bowl would work with furnishings of a different style. We simply decided where it would look best. Oftentimes, this is how easy it can be. Sometimes, however, it can necessitate more planning.

Before I offer more detailed advice on decorating using this approach, it is important to understand that this kind of decorating usually appeals to one of two different personalities: the "collector" and the "eclectic." Both personalities love the look created by combining items of different styles, but for different reasons. And their ultimate goals for their finished decors often differ as well.

OPPOSITE **This graceful living room is an exotic mix of elements from many different styles: African and modern art are showcased among Portuguese furniture and Mediterranean-inspired architecture. What I think is most successful about this room is the way it reflects who my clients are: world travelers and devoted art collectors.**

The Collector

THE "COLLECTOR" purchases art and accessories with a certain degree of seriousness. They always seem to be on the lookout for great finds to add to their home, whether they are acquired through travel or visits to flea markets, antique shops, galleries, and auctions. Their style, shape, or size generally does not matter to the collector. They can be 100 years old or contemporary reproductions. For a collector, the most important aspect of art or an antique is that each item represents a story and that it has character.

The story of the pieces they collect can be related to where they were made, the material they're made from, or the artist or artisan who made it. The collector is interested in imbuing a room with the unique quality the piece represents. And heirlooms are particular favorites of collectors because of the family relationships they symbolize. A decor created using this approach very much gives you a sense of the person who lives there.

Over the years, I have had the great privilege of working with many clients who are collectors of everything from glass art to ivory miniatures to snuff boxes. Their passion for the art that beautifies their homes has been inspiring.

If you are a collector, you need to be careful that your collectibles don't overwhelm the room. With so many items of different colors, textures, and materials, the effect can feel cluttered and unrefined. The collection should be inviting to guests, not make them feel like they are visiting a flea market. One surefire way to know if your collectibles have taken over is by listening to guests' comments. If you routinely hear one of the following, I would advise you to rethink what's in the room:

- Wow, this is interesting.
- I've never seen anything like it.
- How long did it take you to collect all of these things?
- I don't think you can add one more thing!

Having a collection of extraordinary objects can be the springboard for great design, but there is a right way and a wrong way to do it. To avoid the comments above, other features in the room should be understated. I recommend:

- Floors and walls should have very little pattern or no pattern at all.
- Fabrics should be predominantly solid colors, though some accent items can have prints.
- Use fully upholstered seating—don't distract the eye by combining too many materials on a single piece of furniture.
- Use good artificial lighting to brighten the room and highlight special items.

If your collection is small or if you collect one type of object, such as porcelain figurines, it's best to find—or design—a piece of furniture where you can showcase the collection, such as a cabinet or wall unit. Otherwise, the collection may get lost among the other items in the room or seem out of place.

BELOW **My client collects glass art, and in this family room where everyone relaxes and watches TV, I created a custom wall unit to display it. If you have a similar collection, in which the objects tend to be small, it's best to feature them together in a wall unit or cabinet.**

OPPOSITE **A collection of treasured objects doesn't have to be large enough to fill a museum. This cherry-wood curio cabinet owned by Latonya and Samuel L. Jackson houses a small group of collectibles that has been in her family for three generations.**

The Eclectic

THE "ECLECTIC" mixes furnishings of different styles and periods for very different reasons than the collector. Their aim in employing this approach to decorating is to achieve a certain aesthetic, and they don't incorporate items into their decor because they are conversation pieces. They respond to an object because of the way it looks, not because of what it represents.

Generally, the eclectic purchases new items from stores, rather than from antique shops or flea markets. This does not mean that the design of their home is overly influenced by room groupings on a showroom floor. On the contrary: while they rely on store-bought furnishings for their home, they create a design that expresses their individuality.

The eclectic likes to pull together items from a variety of places to realize their idea. To use the analogy of buying clothes: the eclectic doesn't buy an entire outfit straight off the rack. She's the girl who buys jeans from one store and a lace blouse from another and tops off the outfit with a great necklace from yet another store—and she looks fantastic. She approaches her decorating in the same way: she buy items from different sources and coordinates a cohesive decor with them.

LEFT Regardless of how small an area is in a house, you can still make a statement with its decor. This foyer combines a traditional console with modern art and an African rhythm pounder (far right on the table).

OPPOSITE African and folk art are a passion of mine and I use examples of both throughout my home. In this area just off my kitchen, I have featured an old screen door that has been painted and hung on the wall, an African Ashanti carved bench, and a pair of contemporary bar stools. The stools have gun metal bases and beautiful red ostrich leather upholstery.

ABOVE **This cozy breakfast room combines items in several different styles, including an art deco light fixture, a contemporary table made of acrylic, and transitional chairs.**

OPPOSITE **Set apart from the rest of the house by a series of large columns, this dining room combines transitional chairs and lighting with a contemporary table to create an eclectic decor.**

The old adage "keep it simple" applies to the eclectic approach to decorating. Start by selecting the primary period or style you plan to use. When creating your decor, use this ratio:

- 75–85 percent of the elements in a room should reflect your primary period or style
- 15–25 percent can be of a different period or style

When considering items to mix with your primary period or style, I suggest using the following:

- End tables or accent tables
- Light fixtures
- Framed mirrors
- Side chairs
- Wall consoles
- Area rugs

Trying to create an eclectic look using only accessories—such as vintage candlesticks, picture frames, throw pillows, and wall art—is not sufficient. Larger pieces are needed to successfully create your decor. You should, however, incorporate accessories as accents.

OPPOSITE **In this eclectic room, I used two French chairs in the predominantly contemporary-style home. When trying to create an eclectic design, select the primary style of the home (in this case it's contemporary) and add just a few elements from a different style or period (the French chairs).**

STEP
5
Let's Review

Combining different styles in a decor may seem like it requires the help of a professional, but great results are achievable by the novice decorator. Typically this look appeals to two types of personalities: the collector and the eclectic. One of the first things you will need to do is determine which personality type best describes you. With that information, it will be much easier for you to successfully create a beautiful design that reflects your tastes.

THE COLLECTOR
The collector is always looking to add fascinating and unique pieces to their home. Their collections generally consist of art and accessories, and collectors tend to add items to their collections because of what the piece represents or symbolizes.

One of the challenges with this approach to decorating is making sure the collection does not overwhelm the room. Because pieces in the collection will be in a variety of colors and textures, the rest of the room decor should be relatively simple, so minimize the use of pattern and use solid colors for fabric upholstery. And be sure to highlight the collection with artificial lighting whenever possible.

THE ECLECTIC
The eclectic personality loves combining styles and periods as a way to achieve a desired look or aesthetic and not because the items within the decor are conversation pieces. Unlike the collector, the eclectic usually purchases new items from stores rather than acquiring them during travel or on trips to galleries and antique stores. This doesn't mean, however, that they will want to purchase their decor straight from a showroom model or sales brochure, as they want to create a design that reflects their taste. If you are an eclectic, use the following ratio when creating your decor:

- 75–85 percent of the elements in a room should reflect your primary period or style
- 15–25 percent can be of a different period or style

Choose Your Colors

Welcome to the wonderful world of color! We all know how important color is in our surroundings. The rich reds and luminous yellows of flowers, the bright greens of grass, the vibrant blues of the sea and sky—they all have an immediate and positive impact on our mood. There is no greater enhancement to an interior design than the addition of color. Our demanding lives make it even more critical to create a home that gives us pleasure, and I have always relied on color to do just that.

There are many theories on color and how it affects us. New studies are conducted every day, and many industries use color therapy with encouraging results. For example, hospitals and nursing homes use certain colors because it is believed they help the healing process; office buildings, schools, and libraries use color to aid concentration; in restaurants color is used to stimulate appetite; and even in department stores color is used to encourage impulse buying. Product development and packaging has been greatly influenced by studies on how color affects consumer spending habits. As you can see, color is very much of interest to a broad range of disciplines.

Most experts in the field of color perception believe that color can elicit emotional, behavioral, and even physiological changes in human beings. As a result of much research, different colors have been ascribed certain characteristics.

Without really knowing why, many of us find ourselves drawn to certain colors and combinations of colors, and these preferences will shape the interiors that we design for ourselves. This brief introduction about the effect color has on our bodies and minds will be helpful as you determine the kind of feeling you want to create in your home. Following is a list of eight colors and their attributes.

OPPOSITE **I don't shy away from color for my clients' homes or my own—and my guest room, which combines several vibrant colors with neutral tones, is an explosion of color. The red, yellow, blue, and green colors featured in the framed artwork can be found in the mirrored coverlet that is used as a bedspread. The throw pillows were made from the fabric of a treasured Indian sari, and the night table adds the finishing touch to this exotic decor.** PHOTOGRAPHY BY KIM SARGENT. COURTESY ARCHITECTURAL DIGEST. ©2004. THE CONDÉ NAST PUBLICATIONS, INC. ALL RIGHTS RESERVED. USED WITH PERMISSION.

Red is the color of love, vitality, courage, and passion. It has been proven to increase heart rate and respiration, to aid digestion, and increase strength. Red can be perceived as hot, sexy, aggressive, impulsive, and sensual.

Orange is an active, cheerful, and exuberant color. It has been proven to decrease irritability and hostility and improve social behavior. Orange is perceived to be gregarious, jovial, extroverted, pleasure-seeking, and fickle.

Green is considered the color of growth and refreshment. It has been perceived as the color of envy and jealousy, as well as moderation, tradition, and balance.

Yellow has been associated with happiness, warmth, and optimism, but has also been proven to increase irritability and hostility. It is attributed to sharpening memory, aiding digestion, and stimulating appetite. Yellow has been variously perceived as cautious, introspective, egotistical, innovative, and communicative.

> I have always said that I don't have a favorite color; I like using all colors in a decor as long as they have been properly distributed. I tend to use neutrals on walls and larger upholstery pieces. This allows me to introduce color on the smaller furnishings with upholstery and art without overwhelming the space.

ABOVE, RIGHT, AND OPPOSITE
Examples of beautiful colors: let them inspire you to include more color in your home!

Blue is the color of serenity and peace. It has been proven to lower blood pressure and slow the respiratory rate. Blue can be perceived as cool, relaxing, loyal, astute, responsible, pragmatic, as well as manipulative, dogmatic, and conservative.

Violet is the color of royalty, reverence, and quietness. It has been proven to lower blood pressure, suppress appetite, and quiet overactive glands and organs. Violet can be perceived as the color of elegance, creativity, and spirituality.

Black is considered the color of mourning, mystery, sophistication, and dignity. It can be perceived as worldly, intimidating, powerful, dignified, and aloof.

White is perceived as the color of joy, hope, innocence, and cleanliness. It is associated with purity, enlightenment, and optimism.

Color Has a Place in Your Decor

I AM SURE YOU HAVE SEEN interiors in magazines that only use neutral colors, such as beige, with accents in black or other neutral tones. I find this look cold and stark. I have always believed in the importance of going beyond "safe" neutrals and adding bold, vibrant color to a decor, even if it's just one item like a painting or throw pillows. Color breathes life and vitality into a space, so I encourage you to make it an important feature in your home. And virtually all surfaces and three-dimensional items work well in color.

The purpose of this step is to teach you how to balance color and create good color distribution and flow in a room. I will *not* tell you what colors to select. However, by developing a better awareness of color and an understanding of the principles of balance and distribution when using it, you can incorporate color into your decor with confidence. When you are done, it will look like a professional did it!

The red accent wall in this contemporary family room balances perfectly with the two leather club chairs in the room (in the foreground). Using white walls and cabinetry ensured that the room was not overwhelmed with red, which is a heavy color.

Color flow is one of the most important concepts when using color in an interior. Color flow occurs when your eye follows color easily around the room. If your eye becomes fixated on one item or area in the room to the exclusion of all else, you have not achieved color flow.

Simple Rules for Color Distribution and Balance

Rule #1 Color in a room should be found throughout the room, not just on one item. Whatever color is on the right side of the room, place a touch of it on the left. If the color is on both the left and right sides of the room, add a touch of it in the middle. "Touches" of color can be added with accent pillows and throw blankets, for example. The objective is to create continuity, or flow, among the furnishings and accessories in a room.

Rule #2 Use a maximum of three colors per room. This does not apply to shades of a color, nor does it apply to neutrals, such as white, beige, black, gray, and brown. Hard-surface items such as tables, consoles, or wood items are generally considered neutrals.

Rule #3 Select one color that can be used throughout several rooms in your home. This will pull the entire decorating scheme together. Otherwise, you may have a series of beautiful rooms that don't seem to cohere overall.

Ty Law's billiard room has a sports-inspired theme, so I used red, blue, and gray as the primary colors. The custom carpet has blue and red patterns carved into a gray background. The same colors can be found in the framed football jerseys and memorabilia, which leave no doubt that Law was a football player for the New England Patriots.

This is one of the many incarnations of my bedroom. I chose a white theme—I used it for my bedding, wallcoverings, carpeting, and window treatments—because I knew that would best showcase the large painting above my bed.

Color balance is governed by how colors of various "weights" are used in a room. The weight of color is determined by how dark or intense it is. Heavy colors include red, dark yellow, green, blue, purple, and neutrals like black, brown, and charcoal gray. Colors and darker neutrals that are composed 75 percent of a light color (most often white or beige) are light to medium weight. Light neutrals and colors with a high percentage of white (greater than 75 percent) are lightweight.

A room is properly color balanced if:

- It does not appear to "tilt" (i.e., one area of the room does not have too much of a heavy color)
- No one item stands out

The Color Selection Process

COLOR SELECTION is a very personal decision. What appeals to you may not appeal to someone else, but this does not mean that there is a right or wrong color selection. What matters is how you use the colors you've chosen.

To begin, try to visualize your room without color. You need to see the forms of the furnishings, walls, window treatments, and ceiling in black and white before you can think about color placement. I learned this helpful technique in art school when we were taught about color balance.

To do this, pretend you are an artist and think of your floor plan as a black-and-white composition. Now, begin to select colors and the location of colors for each form. It's the colors you select, and their distribution throughout the room, that creates a flow and balance in the total composition.

But what will be very important when making those decisions, is the order in which you determine where color will go, because the color of certain features in your room will determine the color of other features. Choose the color for these items in the following order:

1 Flooring and floor coverings
2 Upholstery fabrics
3 Window treatments and wallcoverings

FLOORING

The first color selection you should make for a room is the flooring. The color will, of course, be determined by the type of flooring you choose. You should begin here, because it establishes the character of a room and is the foundation of the room's design.

Floors that are light or neutral colors are very easy to coordinate with decorative items. By contrast, dark or bright flooring and floor coverings with a heavy texture or inlaid design will be far more prominent and make a greater impact on the room. If you choose dark or bright flooring, you will always have to consider its color when selecting decorative items and wallcoverings, so think carefully before you make a final decision. Believe me, the last thing you want is to regret your decision regarding the color of flooring. You can rearrange furniture and accessories, and you can change the color of a wall, but in most cases you cannot change the color of a floor without replacing it.

Carpet warms up a room, and carpet in neutral colors remains the most popular choice for most homeowners. Using beige carpet in this room was the best selection for the romantic look I wanted to achieve. The dark wood of the furnishings contrasts beautifully with the soft beiges of the walls, window treatment, bedding, and upholstery.

Let me take a moment here and tell you about a job I did in 1977. You can imagine how memorable it was since I remember the exact date. Unfortunately, it wasn't memorable for the reasons one would like, or at least, it wasn't at the beginning. My client had just purchased a condominium with lime green shag carpeting. She didn't love the color, but she wasn't willing to spend the money to change it. I was horrified. When you walked into the room, all you could see was the carpeting. When I started on the project, I had no idea how I was going to work around it.

Before long, though, I had a plan and within two months the room was finished, green carpet and all. If I do say so myself, it was beautiful. How did I do it? I installed wallpaper with small, light patterns that had touches of green. I brought in solid-colored, fully upholstered seating to cover large areas of the carpet. The end result was that the walls and the furniture directed your eyes up, not down, because I wanted to deflect attention away from the carpet as much as possible. I hope you don't have a floor covering as difficult to overcome as lime green shag carpeting, but if you do, this method of redirecting the viewer's eye away from it will work very well.

LEFT **Ceramic tile is one of the popular choices for flooring because it's durable and affordably priced. In this home bar, it coordinates well with the concrete countertop and the light-colored upholstery on the bar stools.**

OPPOSITE **My celebrity client's lakefront hideaway has a lovely view of the waterfront as soon as you enter the door, and the foyer's design reminds you of this with its glass mosaic tile in brilliant blues and greens installed to look like flowing water.**

If you are lucky enough to be able to choose your own flooring, be aware of any adjoining flooring. While in principle it is acceptable to have different colors and types of flooring in different rooms of a house, there is a possibility it won't look good. This is especially true for carpeting. For example, let's suppose you have three bedrooms and a hallway located in the same area of your home, and that the carpeting in each room and the hallway are different colors. Four different colors of carpeting in the same area can look like a remnant sale. Using this example as a case study, there are two possible solutions to the problem:

- Find a tweed carpet that contains all the colors in the bedroom carpets and use it in the hallway.
- Use the same neutral carpeting in the bedrooms, but add a border to it in the color of choice for that room. Use the neutral carpeting without the border in the hallway.

Finally, it is generally considered wise to limit yourself to a maximum of three or four different types of flooring in your home. For example, you can use hardwood flooring in the main living areas, carpeting in the bedrooms, and tile in the bath and kitchen areas.

UPHOLSTERY FABRICS

The color of upholstery is not only important because it is a major component of the room's design, but also because the color of the fabric is related to its durability—certain colors wear better than others. Generally, darker colors wear better than lighter colors. When selecting colors for your upholstery, use your furniture plan to help you visualize the size of the upholstered piece. The size of the furniture will determine how strong the color's presence will feel in a room.

BELOW, LEFT **Small inlay details are a great option when you want to add a creative element to your flooring, and they can also add accents of color picked up from elsewhere in the room to help with color balance and flow.**

BELOW, RIGHT **Leather is an unusual choice for flooring, but it can be very handsome, as it is in this home office, and it wears beautifully over time.**

Contrary to popular belief, you can walk on glass tile, which I installed in this cabana bathroom. I used primarily blue tiles and combined them with smaller tiles in bright greens, purples, and other colors in geometric patterns.

CREATING COLOR BALANCE These four diagrams illustrate both the right and wrong ways to balance color in a room.
1 One heavy color in a room full of light colors looks out of place.
2 Too much heavy color in one area of a room makes a room "tilt," or look unbalanced.
3 A single heavy color used on most of the furnishings feels much too strong and overwhelming for a room.
4 Finally, perfect color balance. The two primary colors used in the room are used on different furnishings and are combined to upholster the bench and make throw pillows.

The effect of a small, crimson red ottoman and a large, crimson red modular sofa will be completely different, for example. Another way to anticipate how the finished piece will look is to use my Get It Right! Furniture Patterns, arrange them in the room, and lay your fabric swatches on them. I recommend this approach because most people have trouble visualizing furniture to scale, which is critical when you are making color selections.

While I caution you about the effect of bold colors on large pieces of furniture, I don't mean to suggest that you should avoid them. If you do choose to use bold colors, however, you should be sure to balance that piece of furniture with other pieces that are not bold or vibrant. The same is true if you have dark colors: if you choose a black sofa, choose a lighter color for the chairs in the room to create balance.

When trying to achieve good color balance among furnishings in a room, keep in mind that this is determined by:
1 The size of the item
2 The location of the item
3 The intensity of the color

I must admit that professional interior designers have a big advantage over retail shoppers when it comes to the issue of color balance, because of our access to design centers where fabrics and furniture are sold separately. This allows us to choose any fabric they offer and use it on any piece of furniture they sell. (A list of design centers arond the country is in the Sources section on page 174.)

1 WRONG

2 WRONG

3 WRONG

4 RIGHT!

However, some stores do offer a choice of upholstery for their furniture selections. If you do find a store that offers this, ask the salesperson if they have fabric swatches that you can take home with you. It's always preferable to look at the fabric in the room you plan to use it, even if it is a small swatch. Here are a few more suggestions to make sure you choose the right color fabric for your furniture:

1 Take a close-up photo of your fabric selection, and be sure to label it with the item you plan to use the fabric on.
2 Pick up a paint fan from your local paint store. (A paint fan has color chips of every color the store carries.) Take the fan shopping with you and match the color of the items you want to purchase with one of the color chips. This will provide you with something nearly as useful as a fabric swatch.

I know this seems like a lot of work, but creating a beautiful interior design doesn't come easily. Think about it like this: if you are going out for a jog, it takes you 10 minutes to get dressed. If you are going out to an exclusive party, it will take you two hours to get dressed. And decorating your home, like preparing for a big night out, requires some effort.

For those of you who are concerned about making the wrong decision about color in your decor, I suggest you use neutral colors on large items such as sofas, and save the color for smaller items. If you have a penchant for bold, vibrant colors, such as red or green, but don't want your space to be dominated by them, add a pillow or a vase in that color.

I once designed a house for a client who insisted on using a color scheme based on her favorite colors: red, purple, and blue (see the photo on page 124). I chose to use white for the walls, ceiling, and floor. Large seating (such as the sofa) was also covered with white. Three small barrel bar stools were covered in purple. One large chair had a small print with all three colors. The custom area rug was white with ribbonlike flourishes in the three colors. Finally, small, red accent accessories were added to create balance. When you look at the room, the majority of the space is white, but what you see is the color.

Lots of bright colors are combined masterfully in this living room: I used mint green on the walls, bright pink fabric on the sofa, and a patterned fabric on the club chair and throw pillows that picks up all the colors in the room.

BELOW The art, color scheme, and rounded shapes of the sofas and coffee tables give this living room a feeling of whimsy and playfulness. The custom area rug unites all the colors in the room. Its design was inspired by the lifesize sculpture of a painter on the back wall.

OPPOSITE This room is a great example of proper color distribution, flow, and balance. The eye moves easily over the red and gold fabric in the club chair and throw pillows on the sofa and finds touches of those colors throughout the room: in the flower, the book on the coffee table, and the art.

WINDOW TREATMENTS AND WALLCOVERINGS

When I am designing a room, many times I select my window treatments and wallcoverings last, even though wallcoverings are generally the second items to be installed after flooring in a new home or during a renovation. But at this stage, we are discussing the order in which the color is *chosen* for the various elements within a home, not the order in which these elements are installed.

The reason I select the color of wallcoverings and window treatments last is because they can often resolve color balance problems. While the colors of upholstery fabrics are limited by furniture manufacturers, fabrics for window treatments are only limited by the selection of a fabric store (which is generally extensive), and wallcoverings, particularly paint, are available in a huge variety. So be sure to bring your upholstery fabric with you when you shop for window treatments to ensure a perfect match.

Putting It All Into Practice

BY THIS POINT, you should have all your sample colors and fabric and paint swatches. Spread them out and arrange them so you have a good sense if they will all work together. If you are unsure about your selections, look at this chapter again and study the photos to see how I was able to create good color balance and distribution in my interiors. Pay attention to how your eye travels around the room. You want to avoid using any color—regardless of what item it's on—that dominates the room or demands your attention. The objective is for the eye to travel easily from one item or feature to the next.

6

Let's Review

Your color preferences will play a large role in determining the colors you select for your decor. Whatever colors you ultimately choose, however, the process by which you create color balance and flow in your decor will be the same.

- **VISUALIZE YOUR ROOM IN BLACK AND WHITE** Begin the process of selecting color by not thinking about it—at least at first. Think of your room as a blank canvas. Before you apply any color to this canvas, you need to have a good sketch of the composition, which is your furniture plan. With your furniture plan in front of you, you can then think about where to place color.

- **CHOOSE COLORS FOR YOUR SPACE** You should choose the color of various elements in a room in a certain order:

  1 **Flooring and floor coverings** If you don't have existing flooring and are able to choose it, remember that neutrals are easy to coordinate with other decorative items, while dark or bright colors may require more effort.

  2 **Upholstery fabrics** The size of the furniture will be important when you make a decision regarding color.

  3 **Window treatments and wallcoverings** When shopping for these items, be sure to bring swatches of your upholstery fabric to make sure they coordinate with each other.

My advice for nonprofessionals is to limit yourself to three colors per room. Neutrals—such as black, white, beige, or brown—do not count toward the maximum of three colors, nor do shades of any of the three colors. To create a design that feels cohesive throughout the house, I suggest that you have one color that can be found in every room.

Use a Variety of Fabric Patterns and Textures

I am sure many of you have admired gorgeous and tasteful interiors in magazines that combine decorative items with many different patterns and textures. These rooms often remind me of my grandmother's handmade quilts. I was always impressed by her ability to know what patches of fabric would look great next to each other. It takes some talent and skill to create a successful interior design in a room using a variety of fabric patterns and textures.

Consider the room pictured on pages 128–129. The sofa is upholstered in a fabric with large pink and purple flowers with flowing green and yellow leaves, and it is paired with two wood-frame French chairs covered in a different floral design (although with similar colors and shades). There are two barrel chairs with a striped pattern in green, pink, and white. Antique tapestry-stitch patterns in yellow, purple, and pink adorn two footstools, and a white embossed fabric covers another large sofa. This sofa is accessorized with throw pillows in purple, green, and pink, whose trim picks up the colors found in the floral sofa fabric. And, to top it off, all of these patterns share the same space with an area rug with a large floral motif in green, purple, and pink against a white background.

I believe that all rooms have more character when pattern is a part of the decor. Some well-designed rooms depend upon art and accessories to add pattern, while others rely on fabrics. In this chapter I will focus on combining pattern and texture in a room using various fabrics.

OPPOSITE **Bright and cheerful colors make up the many fabric patterns in this sitting room located off a master bedroom. The white wall provides a neutral backdrop to the large, medium, and small patterns in the window treatments, sofa, and rug.**

This light-filled living room mixes patterns successfully because every pattern used features the same colors. In addition to several patterns of different sizes and colors, the room features a white sofa with texture. The custom area rug carries the largest pattern in the room.

1 PILLOW

2 PILLOW

3 SOFA

7 CHAIR

6 CHAIR

5 SOFA

4 PILLOW

Five Rules for Mixing Patterns and Textures

I REALIZE MANY PEOPLE avoid this approach to decorating, because it is intimidating. With a little guidance and my five rules, however, you will be able to incorporate multiple patterns to bring richness and variety to your decor. The five rules are:

1 Control color and shade
2 Control pattern size
3 The size of the item determines the pattern size
4 Some patterns don't mix
5 Combine patterns with solid colors

Before we go further, I need to distinguish between pattern and texture. For our purposes, a pattern is a design motif sufficiently large enough or with enough color contrast for the eye to see it clearly. Patterns that are very subtle, small, or nearly imperceptible are considered textures rather than patterns.

To begin, choose a fabric with a bold or medium motif. The fabric must have at least three colors or two colors and a shade of one of the colors. Are you sure you love it? Good, because this pattern will be what I call your "lead" fabric and will be used to determine all the other colors, patterns, and textures in your room.

Relying on a lead fabric is one of the best and easiest methods for selecting colors for your home and making sure that fabrics, wallcoverings, and flooring match. Companies who design and manufacture upholstery fabrics often use professional artists to create the color palettes of the patterned fabric they make, which means that some of the work deciding what colors coordinate well is already done for you.

Now let's get back to the five rules for combining patterns and discuss them in more depth.

> I always use a lead fabric in my interiors because it saves time. For the beginner, it will not only make it easier to select coordinating fabrics, it will ensure that your color selections based on the lead fabric will work together. Before a fabric goes into production, the manufacturer has already spent lots of money determining which color combinations look best, so, if the fabric makes it to market, you can guarantee that the color combination is both tasteful and appealing.

CONTROL COLOR AND SHADE

The reason the lead fabric must have three colors is because you will be choosing items to place throughout the room in those three colors. To determine what those colors are, closely study the lead fabric. This is very important because one color can come in many different shades. The secret to combining patterns is to make sure the colors used in the other patterned or solid-colored items are identical to those in your lead fabric. The eye enjoys visual continuity and colors that match. This color continuity will allow you to change patterns without sacrificing an overall sense of harmony.

CONTROL PATTERN SIZE

The size and boldness of the motifs or colors in a pattern greatly affect whether you perceive the room to be too "busy" or pleasing to the eye. And the size of the space dictates not only the number of patterns a room should have, but also what size the pattern should be. Generally, large patterns work well in large rooms, and small patterns work in small rooms (large patterns in neutral colors also work in small rooms).

Large floral patterns don't have to overwhelm a room. Using a pattern with a light or neutral background, as in this living room, ensures that the pattern is not too bold or heavy for the decor. Neutrals or medium neutrals tend to tone down large patterns.

One way to determine if you are in "pattern overload" is to pay attention to your immediate reaction when entering a room. Are all patterns located in one area in the room? Are most of the patterns bold? If so, you may have too much pattern in the room.

To avoid this, you should use the following:

- One large, bold pattern
- Two medium-size patterns in medium-weight colors
- Four to five small patterns

In a bold fabric pattern the motif or lines in the design dominate every part of the fabric and the colors are not muted. In a medium-size pattern, the colors are noticeable but, in most cases, do not cover every part of the fabric. Motifs and lines tend to be tighter and more repetitive. Small patterns are generally so small they appear to be woven, not printed. Woven fabrics would also be characterized as small patterns. In both cases, the pattern is very faint. Patterns that are composed of neutral colors or tone-on-tone patterns are also considered small patterns because of their ability to blend.

THE SIZE OF THE ITEM DETERMINES THE PATTERN SIZE

As discussed above, large rooms can very easily accommodate large patterns. Most of us, however, live in average-size spaces. As someone new to interior design, you don't want to use your boldest pattern on the largest item or area in a room, such as wallcoverings, sofas that are 8 feet or longer, or window treatments. Limit your use of bold patterns, because people tend to tire of them very quickly.

If you plan to reupholster your existing furniture, you should always be aware of how the size of the item affects the pattern repeat (or the entire motif). Most upholstery or window treatment fabrics are 54 inches wide, but others can be 45–60 inches wide. Some furniture items such as living room side chairs may not be wide enough to carry the full repeat of a bold pattern. For example, if your chair is 24 inches wide and your pattern repeat is 27 inches, part of your pattern will need to be trimmed off. No matter how much you love it, this pattern is not a good choice for this application.

The same would be true if the chair is 30 inches wide and the pattern is 24 inches wide. Because the full pattern would not be sufficient to cover it, you would need more fabric, which would mean that there would be a seam on the back and seat of the chair. The seam will make the chair uncomfortable to sit in, and the chair will look like it was not professionally upholstered.

The shape of the item to be upholstered will also determine what pattern to choose. For example, round barrel chairs and striped fabrics don't always work together. Matching stripes on the round backs and the flat of seats of these types of chairs is a difficult task.

When choosing upholstery fabrics, be sure to match the pattern repeat to the size of the piece being covered.

SOME PATTERNS DON'T MIX

Using patterns from very different periods or styles is not recommended. Traditional patterns and modern patterns will not look good together. For example, if your decor features French-country patterns, you should not combine these items with modern geometric patterns. However, various types of fabric with actual texture, such as velvet, damask, brocade, and taffeta, can be combined with informal fabrics such as linen, cotton, and tweed.

COMBINE PATTERNS WITH SOLID COLORS

Balance is essential in any room, but particularly ones that feature several different patterns. The best way to achieve this is to add items with solid colors to the decor. I refer to these items as "neutrals" (though they don't need to be neutral colors).

> When I am working with large, bold patterns, I always use lots of neutrals. They relieve the eye and also make the room look less "busy."

BELOW **The bold patterns set against shades of rich reds of the wallpaper in this handsome dining room (left) and kitchen (right) are balanced by the neutral wood furnishings and white cabinets and molding.**

OPPOSITE **The wallpaper in this dining room may have overwhelmed the room if not for the white wainscoting, which tones it down and provides separation between the pattern and the rest of the room.**

ABOVE **Using neutral colors, as this living room's walls and floor coverings do, is important when you combine several patterns in a room.**
OPPOSITE **In this bedroom, several patterns with predominantly neutral colors are used on the wallcovering, window treatments, and bedding.**

Combining Patterns by Example

Using several rooms from one of the houses I designed, I will show you how to combine patterns. Because the house had an open floor plan, it was even more critical that the patterns coordinated across several distinct but adjoining areas. As you can see in this living room, I used pattern for the chairs (which are upholstered in the lead fabric), sofa, and area rug.

NOW THAT YOU KNOW the rules for this approach to decorating, it's time to start applying these rules to your decor. Still feeling unsure about doing it on your own? No problem. I will take you step by step through the process using one of my interiors as an example.

DETERMINE YOUR LEAD FABRIC

Once you've chosen your lead fabric, use it on an item in the center of the room. I generally use the lead fabric on frame-upholstered chairs. (As I discussed in Step 3, chairs are generally located in conversation groupings, which tend to be in the middle of the room.) You want to use your lead fabric in the center of the room, because this pattern includes all the colors you will use on the other items in the room. In this example, I have used a gorgeous brocade in shades of red, brown, taupe, and beige.

LEFT The lead fabric that determined what colors would be used throughout the various rooms in the house.

BELOW All the fabrics, trims, and materials used in our example decor, including velvet, chenilles, silks, and leather.

RIGHT **In the family room, which can be seen clearly from the living room, I used primarily neutral colors with occasional accents of red in the art and accessories.**

BELOW, LEFT **The game room features upholstery in beige and taupe.**

BELOW, RIGHT **Different shades of red, beige, and taupe are used in the dining room, which are all derived from the lead fabric.**

ADD NEUTRAL COLORS

In our example, I upholstered the sofa in the living room (page 138) in a neutral from the lead fabric. The sofa is beige chenille, which is the same shade as the background of our fabric.

ADD ACCENT COLORS

I used throw pillows in three different patterns and put them on the sofa: brown silk with woven dots of red, brown, and pink; red velvet with a woven leaf in shades of red and gold; and red silk with woven gold leaves. The colors found on these accents are all taken from the lead fabric. In addition, a sumptuous velvet throw blanket is used on the sofa. For added interest, I covered the bench in the window in a woven fabric with a small print of red and taupe.

Note that I chose beige for the walls and another neutral for the window treatments, which visually connect the eye with the beige sofa. To pull the entire look together, I used an area rug with all the colors from our lead fabric woven in a subtle design.

It's also important to note that this home has an open floor plan. There are four rooms that open into each other: the game area, dining room, family room, and living room. The lead-fabric colors are used throughout each of the rooms, so that the look overall is harmonious.

STEP 7

Let's Review

Most people feel intimidated about combining different patterns in their decor, because they think it is difficult to do well. But if you follow my five simple rules, you can do it so that your space looks well balanced and not overwhelmed by pattern. The rules are:

1 Control color and shade
2 Control pattern size
3 The size of the item determines the pattern size
4 Some patterns don't mix
5 Combine patterns with solid colors

Determining which patterns to combine is made much simpler if you use a lead fabric. A lead fabric is a bold or medium pattern that should be comprised of no more than three colors. The other decorative items you incorporate into the room—both patterned and solid-colored—should have these three colors in them.

The number of different patterns you use is important. My advice is to limit yourself to one large, bold pattern; two medium-size patterns in medium colors; and four to five small patterns. The boldest pattern should not be on the largest item or area in the room, so avoid using it on wallcoverings, window treatments, or sofas.

If you are still unsure about how to go about combining pattern, follow these steps:

1 Select a lead fabric and use it in the center of the room.
2 Add neutral colors and locate them on large items such as sofas, walls, and window coverings. (If your lead fabric has neutral colors, use those. Otherwise, choose a neutral that works with your color scheme.)
3 Add accents, such as throw rugs, throw pillows, trims, or artwork, in the three colors from the lead fabric to create color flow.

STEP 8
Decorate with Art and Accessories

If there is one step in my nine-step process that really makes a house a home, this is it. If you skip it, you may still have a lovely decor, but in my opinion it will always feel unfinished. If you doubt how crucial art and accessories are to the overall effect of a space, consider this: even cavemen understood that art was a vital part of their dwellings. By drawing and etching on their cave walls, they gave their immediate surroundings a spirit.

I love the line in *Steel Magnolias* when Clairee says, "Honey, the only thing that separates us from the animals is our ability to accessorize!" I couldn't agree more. I feel so strongly about the importance of art and accessories that I include consignment art and accessories in all of my decorative installations to show clients how fantastic a properly accessorized home looks. Most of my clients are so impressed that they generally keep 80 percent of the pieces I have used. This is not only because I know how to pick the right items, but because at that point, they really understand what a positive impact these items have on an interior design. Not only does art create a mood and endow a space with personality, it can also coordinate elements in a decor.

As I have said, balance is the key to a decor that looks like it was created by a professional. By the time you reach this step, you've created balance among various elements—including the furniture arrangement and the colors and patterns used—to make the room sing. I use the word "sing" because all of these selections have created a rhythm and beat that define the space. And if you follow the lead of that beat as you add art and accessories, it will be like adding a complementary melody to an already beautiful song.

OPPOSITE **Art is one of the most important features in a great interior design. For these clients, I created long rectangular niches for them to display their extensive art collection.**

Types of Art and Accessories

TO MAKE SHOPPING for art and accessories easy, I have categorized the most common of these items and they include: items for tabletops and other surfaces, items for the floor, items for walls, items placed on furnishings, and collectibles. Obviously, this is just a sampling of the art and accessories you can use in your home, but hopefully this will give you some idea of the many choices you have.

1 ITEMS FOR TABLETOPS AND OTHER SURFACES

Vases
Bowls
Dishes
Boxes
Candles and candlesticks
Books
Sculptures
Lamps
Trays
Picture frames
Bottles
Flowers and plants
Clocks
Planters
Urns
Baskets

2 ITEMS FOR THE FLOOR

Sculpture
Plants and greenery
Urns
Clocks
Lamps
Large mirrors
Area rugs
Baskets
Candles and candleholders

3 ITEMS FOR WALLS

Paintings and prints
Sculptures
Sconces
Photographs
Fiber art/textiles (including rugs)
Framed mirrors
Candleholders
Wood carvings
Dishes
Architectural elements (such as brackets and corbels)

4 ITEMS PLACED ON FURNISHINGS

Throw pillows
Throw blankets
Runners

5 COLLECTIBLES

Porcelain
Artifacts
Shells
Gems and stones
Finials
Brushes
Pins
Letter openers
Pipes

RIGHT **Small, inexpensive art can be enhanced when it is hung on walls painted with dark, rich colors.**

OPPOSITE **In this contemporary dining room in my client's Manhattan home, I paired a silver-leafed table, modern high-back upholstered chairs, and a pair of Roy Lichtenstein prints.**

What's Your Look?

THERE ARE TWO DISTINCTIVE LOOKS that you can achieve when accessorizing: crafty and artistic. How are they different? Skilled artists and artisans create works of art in pottery, wood, ceramic, as well as paint on canvas and sculpture in various metals. On the other hand, crafts, such as needlepoint, are not the work of a skilled artisan, but rather the hobbyist or amateur. Craft has a handmade feel, while art looks like it belongs in a gallery. The professional interior designer tries to create an artistic look, with a hint of the crafty as well. More often than not, the decors you admire in magazines strike this balance.

As I have repeated throughout this book, sometimes there *is* too much of a good thing! This room (top) has been accessorized on a budget with many hand-crafted items, including needlepoint pillows and pictures; crocheted doilies in various sizes, shapes, and colors; a hooked wall hanging in a vibrant red; a hand-painted wooden box; braided straw flowers in multiple colors; and silk plants and wreaths. The result is colorful, but too fussy and can be improved. With just a few changes, the same room takes on a completely different appearance (bottom). I've kept the major pieces: the sofa, area rug, coffee table, wicker chair, and display stand. And I've also kept selected hand-crafted items: the two needle-point pillows and the wooden box. Adding a large club chair, two framed prints, a few pieces of art glass, and two throw pillows in colors that pick up the border on the area rug has helped considerably. I've also replaced the silk plants with two live ferns, an arrangement of fresh flowers, and a bowl of apples. The result is still colorful, but much more focused and polished.

For those who have mastered a craft and want to display it, such as macramé or tole painting, you will have to be careful not to overwhelm the room with lots of examples of your work. I realize it's tempting to show guests your creative side, but do that through other elements of your decorating.

Art and accessories are now available for all budgets, so even if you don't have a lot of money to spare for this part of your decor, you should be able to add just a few items to enhance the overall look of the room. One of my favorite budget-conscious ways to create a beautiful piece of art is to use custom framing. If you take an inexpensive poster or painting and frame it with a gorgeous frame, you've just significantly increased the perceived value of that art. (If the art seems too small for the wall, you might want to consider painting the wall with a dark color, because it will make the artwork "pop.") There are also many manufacturers of good but inexpensive art replicas that even the smallest of budgets can afford.

I recommend that you shop for larger accessories first, including vases, decorative boxes, and lamps. These items occupy more space and are helpful when trying to create balance. You can always fill in the gaps with smaller items later, if necessary.

A room looks its best when it features a variety of art and accessories, and as you can see in this master bedroom, you can create an understated and sophisticated look by using the appropriate accessories. The warm wood tones and natural fabrics are enlivened by four small paintings, a pair of urns, vases with fresh flowers, and contrasting throw pillows.

Tabletop Art and Accessories

TABLETOP ACCESSORIES should not be confused with wall unit accessories. Wall unit accessories may include collections of items you want to showcase. These items can be displayed in a single line or they can fill the entire wall unit, because you and your guests will not expect to rest items such as drinking glasses or television remotes on a display cabinet.

Tabletop accessories, on the other hand, need to be considered in conjunction with the function of the table. These items should work to create balance on the table and in the room, but keep in mind that balance doesn't matter if the table doesn't serve your needs.

> Regardless of the size of your dining room table, be sure to accessorize it, even with just one item. It can be charming and simple—such as a large wooden bowl filled with colorful fruit—or lavish and dramatic, such as a centerpiece brimming with elegant flowers flanked by tall candlesticks.

DINING TABLE ACCESSORIES

Dining tables are one of the easiest tabletops to accessorize, and it can be as simple as using a single item in the middle of the table. If you choose this approach, the accessory should be approximately one-quarter of either the width or length of the table. The shape and size of your tabletop, not to mention its style, will determine your selection. A variety of containers can be used, such as bowls, dishes, boxes, baskets, and trays, and they can be filled with a range of items to bring color, texture, and fragrance to the table, such as:

Flowers

Fruit, such as apples or oranges

Nuts in the shell

Coconuts with the green husk or brown shell

Gems, stones, rock glass, and shells

Balls made of stone, plastic, metal, wood, paper, or fabric

Candy (only use candies that are wrapped)

Dried items, such as flowers, stems, fruit, roots, leaves, and potpourri

ABOVE **I used an earthenware bowl with bright green apples and a bed of leaves on this small dining room table.**

RIGHT **A floral arrangement in a beautiful vase is a fantastic accessory for the dining room table.**

OPPOSITE **This dining table could have been decorated with the centerpiece alone to create a striking arrangement.**

COFFEE TABLE ACCESSORIES

Accessorizing your coffee table is very important, because it is often in the middle of your room. The eye naturally gravitates there first, so it needs to look great. Personally, it's my favorite surface to accessorize. I frequently save coffee table arrangements for my final decorating flourish.

As important as coffee table decorations are to the overall impression of a room, most people don't get it right, so I have developed a few rules and a list of do's and don'ts to ensure you won't make any mistakes.

Accessories on the coffee table must be of at least three different heights. The height of the tallest item will depend on your ceiling height. In rooms with 12-foot or higher ceilings, the tallest item should be 30–42 inches high. In rooms with 10-foot ceilings, the tallest item should be between 18–24 inches high.

Tall vases with flowers work well in rooms with high ceilings. If you decide to try this, the vase should be 18–24 inches high, and with flowers the total height of the arrangement should be 30–42 inches high. If you have an average-size room and you would like to decorate it with a vase and flowers, the arrangement should be 18–24 inches high. Other tall items you can use on a coffee table are a sculpture, an urn, or a pair of candlesticks.

Medium-height accessories can include a bowl, decorative box, or stack of illustrated books to balance the tall item. I recommend that these accessories be 4–8 inches high. Low items can include dishes, sculptures, and trays. These items should be under 3 inches high.

When accessorizing coffee tables, end tables, and consoles, work with an uneven number of items. For the average-size coffee table, which is approximately 30 inches wide by 48 inches long, use three to five accessories. If you use three items as opposed to five, they should be wider or longer.

When accessorizing, keep in mind the following do's and don'ts:

DO'S

- Do make certain that all items look good together.
- Do combine items made from different materials, such as glass, metal, and wood.
- Do include items that have sentimental value or a great story behind them to personalize the table.
- Do have at least one accessory with color, such as flowers.

DON'TS

- Don't place accessories at each corner.
- Don't place accessories in a straight line.
- Don't overcrowd the table.
- Don't place tall accessories in a location of the table that will block the view of a seated guest.

SIDE TABLE, NIGHT TABLE, AND CONSOLE ACCESSORIES

Lamps are great accessories for end tables and consoles. To ensure the proper proportion of the tabletop to the lamp, choose one in which the diameter of the bottom of the shade (usually the largest part) is smaller than the tabletop. For example, if the tabletop is 18 inches wide and the lampshade is 21 inches in diameter, the shade is too large for that table. When using lamps as accessories, always try to use tall lamps. They are much more impressive and provide better illumination.

Accessories on side tables and night tables serve both an aesthetic and functional purpose. Night tables must have enough space for items, such as:

Lamps	Framed photos	Small books
Clocks	Phones	Television remotes

When tables are located against walls, the accessories should be the appropriate size for the tabletop, but you must also consider how they balance with the size of the wall and the art and accessories on the wall, as the eye sees them as one composition. A console, for example, that rests against a 10-by-18-foot wall must have at least one tall accessory, otherwise the proportions of that ensemble will feel incorrect.

Floor Accessories

IN MOST OF THE HOMES I DESIGN, I select hard-surface floors such as ceramic tile, marble, wood, or stone. I use these types of surfaces because they are low maintenance and will generally last a long time. They do, however, often need an area rug to provide warmth, frame furniture arrangements, add color and texture, and control sound.

Area rugs come in a variety of styles, colors, and materials. Rugs (both traditional and contemporary) can be made from natural fibers such as wool and silk. When selecting an area rug for your room, you want to take into consideration the style of the room. A traditional rug will always look good in a contemporary room, but the reverse is not true: contemporary area rugs do not work in a room with traditional furnishings.

Most area rugs are available in standard sizes (in feet): 6 by 9, 8 by 10, 9 by 12, 10 by 14, and 12 by 15. Area rugs to be used for furniture groupings should be no less than three-quarters of the size of the entire grouping. I suggest a minimum perimeter border of 2–3 feet of exposed flooring around the area rug. This ensures people will walk on the flooring and not the rug.

I cannot emphasize enough how important it is to purchase the correct size rug for your furniture grouping. Using the wrong size rug will make the furniture look like it is too large for the space (even though it isn't) or, worse yet, like you couldn't afford to buy a rug big enough for your space! And a rug that is too large makes the space look poorly planned.

Cecil Says

You can create a "custom" area rug on a budget. I suggest using a piece of wall-to-wall carpeting and have a carpet carver bind on a border, either in a traditional pattern or a solid color.

Floor art that is large, such as the American Indian stone sculpture in the foreground, should have its own designated area, otherwise it can overshadow other features of the decor.

PLANTS AND GREENERY

Plants and other types of greenery are always a great choice for an accessory. They bring color and a bit of nature into your space and are affordable for any budget. They can also provide balance to a room by filling in an empty area. Potted trees in rooms with high ceilings will make them seem better proportioned. While live plants are best, those of you who don't have "green thumbs," should look for silk plants. (Nothing is worse than a dead plant in an otherwise gorgeous room.) Try to purchase ones that look real—they are more expensive, but the extra expense is worth it.

THREE-DIMENSIONAL FLOOR ACCESSORIES

Sculptures and large vases or urns should be situated at the end of a room or stand alone. These large items command space and attention, so be sure their placement doesn't overwhelm the room. If they are placed in the appropriate location, they will balance the overall composition.

Floor lamps can be either next to a side table or behind it. Torchère lamps are very popular because they cast their light upward, which provides better illumination.

Wall Art and Accessories

THESE ITEMS SHOULD BE the last accessories to be placed in a room because they tend to direct the eye down and across other items, so it's important that the rest of the decor is finished to assess how your wall art will affect the overall impression. Wall art is also useful in solving color balance problems. For example, you may have two shades of blue in a room that seem to be competing with each other. By adding a painting that has both shades of blue (as well as other colors), the repetition of those colors in the painting makes the decor of the room seem more cohesive.

For those people who don't consider themselves collectors (as I describe in Step 5), but who want to incorporate art into their decor, I recommend choosing one large piece, such as a painting, that will fill nearly your entire wall. Using one piece as opposed to several will simplify your decorating efforts.

Art can often be a great conversation piece, like this unusual painting used on the wall behind a home bar. I chose a cracked-glass counter and lavender chairs to coordinate with the painting's colors.

Regardless of the size of your art, it will frequently share the wall with other accessories. When using more than one accessory on a wall, however, start the arrangement in the middle of the wall and then add items beside or underneath the central grouping.

Some possible combinations of wall art and accessories are:

Paintings and sconces

Relief sculptures, paintings, and sconces

Carved wall brackets and paintings

Textile art and photographs

Framed mirrors, art, and sconces

When you don't know what to decorate a wall with, a framed mirror is one of my favorite choices. If you plan on using just a framed mirror, the frame should be big and dramatic. And, of course, remember that the finish and style must complement the style of the room.

> I love adding art and accessories to walls because you aren't limited to items that need to be functional—it's all about what looks fantastic.

ABOVE **Whenever you are uncertain about what artwork to include in your decor, I recommend that you consider using a framed mirror.**

RIGHT **In this elegant home, I used a recessed alcove (in the background) in the foyer to display one of the pieces of my client's impressive art collection. I painted the alcove with a deep beige and used a spotlight for a touch of sophistication and drama.**

Hanging art in a grouping, as shown here, is a wonderful way to display a collection of similar works.

Accessories Placed on Furnishings

DON'T UNDERESTIMATE THE IMPACT small items such as throw pillows or blankets can have on your decor, as these items can add a final, beautiful touch to a room. Sumptuous fabrics and detailed trims can make a simple pillow look like a work of art. Throws and textiles add color, texture, and pattern when used on the ends, arms, and edges of sofas, chairs, and beds.

Throw pillows and blankets work well on beds as well as sofas. In this bedroom I used Kuba cloth from Africa for the pillows and throws.

Let's Review

This step is very important because art and accessories make a decor look finished, and the good news is that you don't need a lot of either to make a room fantastic.

Art and accessories fall into five categories.

1 Items for tabletops and other surfaces
2 Items for walls
3 Items for the floor
4 Items placed on furnishings
5 Collectibles

When accessorizing, the look you achieve will fall into one of two categories: crafty or artistic. Crafty decorative items feel more handmade, as though they were created by a hobbyist or amateur. Artistic items feel as though they were made by a professional artist.

Here are a few rules to follow when accessorizing:

TABLETOP ART AND ACCESSORIES

- Dining table accessories should be one-quarter of the width or length of the table.
- Items on the coffee table must be three different heights (for the average-size room): tall (18–21 inches), medium (4–8 inches), and low (under 3 inches).
- Groupings of accessories on tabletops should be comprised of an uneven number of items. For the average-size coffee table, 30 by 48 inches, I recommend using three or five items.

FLOOR ART AND ACCESSORIES

- Area rugs should be used on hard-surface floors for warmth and sound control.
- Area rugs should be no less than three-quarters of the size of the conversation groupings, leaving a perimeter border of 2–3 feet of uncovered flooring in a room.
- Plants and other greenery are an inexpensive but attractive addition to a room.
- Large vases, urns, or sculptures should be placed at the end of a room or stand entirely alone.

WALL ART AND ACCESSORIES

- Place these items in a room last.
- If you are not a collector as I have described, I suggest you cover your wall with one large painting or artwork, or several works can be grouped together for impact.

STEP 9

Evaluate Your Finished Design

You have finally reached the most exhilarating step: assessing how well you have achieved beautiful living. I recommend that you reread this chapter when you are done with your decorating, because I have included lots of photos for inspiration.

This may be the hardest step of my process. You've followed my advice and guidance and learned how to create balance in your decor, and now it's time to see how successful your efforts were. You have spent a lot of time learning why an interior works, and you've applied this information to your home. It has been a journey of discovery about what you like and don't like. Now is the moment of truth, literally: you need to be honest about what you've created. I suggest you don't rely too heavily on other people's opinions: frequently this can make your evaluation harder. You need to listen to your instincts: is your design everything you wanted it to be?

But before you start analyzing, I want you to keep a few things in mind. As should be clear by now, I subscribe to Frank Lloyd Wright's familiar adage "Less is more," and it bears repeating here as you begin to look closely at your newly designed space. The eye determines what fits in a decor more easily if there is less "stuff" crowding the composition. At the completion of your decorating project, adding more items will be easier than taking items away. If you do need to make some changes at this point, don't get discouraged—no one gets it right every time, not even the professionals. I jokingly say that I never finish a design project—my clients throw me out! This is because I can always find one last detail that will improve the room.

OPPOSITE **This is one of the many incarnations of my living room. The impressive faux-stone coffee table is the focal point of the room and is accessorized with a planter, a pair of bronze deer, a glass bowl with apples, and art books.**

Before you make your final evaluation, I recommend you follow the same steps I do to evaluate my work:

1 Leave your home for a minimum of eight hours.

2 Whatever you do during those eight hours, don't think about your finished room or rooms.

3 For at least seven hours, don't even think about decorating.

4 One hour before you return to the house, repeat this mantra: "My decorating is only *partially* about me." This is important, because it will allow you to look at your room more objectively.

What do I mean by saying that how you've decorated your space isn't entirely about you? Because what you've done is dependent on a few factors, not just your taste. Here is a list of other things that will greatly influence your interior design:

● Architectural features

● The room's function

● Principles of good interior design (such as balance)

Before you begin to make the final assessment of your finished decor, keep in mind that adding decorative items is generally easier than removing them. In addition, making an accurate evaluation is often quicker when there are fewer items in the room.

BELOW **This large family room combines a variety of fabric patterns with wood furnishings to create an informal but elegant French-country decor that uses the classic provincial color scheme of blue, yellow, and white.**

OPPOSITE **In this detail of the room below, you can see that the fireplace, crowned with a colorful painting, is the perfect focal point.**

Most of us don't have the opportunity to build our houses from the ground up, so you have to work with what you have. And even then, the design of a custom home is affected by building codes, location, climate, and conditions at the building site. There will always be issues that limit the realization of your ideal home.

The room's function will also determine how the finished room looks. You must consider how the room will be used if you are going to avoid making decisions that you will regret later. For example: you would LOVE a big, white silk sofa for your family room. But the reality is that for everyday use, a tan leather sofa will be more practical and more comfortable.

The principles of interior design—or the rules governing proper proportions and balance—are generally accepted by professional designers because they know how important employing these principles is to good design. And we've discussed them at length in this book. So, as you can see, as much as we want to think of our homes as a *complete* reflection of ourselves, it's clear that many other important factors will affect how our decor looks. Knowing this will hopefully make it easier to judge your work. So, back to the task at hand . . .

LEFT **A few different patterns are used in this home. Here, you can see the pattern on the walls and upholstery is identical (though done in different shades of green), and in the adjoining room there is a striped wallcovering, again using the same color scheme.**

OPPOSITE **Many patterns are combined here. The room works because the reds match exactly, and there is a mix of large, medium, and small patterns separated by neutral elements. Also, the patterns are located in several different areas in the room.**

You've been away from your house for the required eight hours. It's time to look at your space with fresh eyes and evaluate. What do you see?

NEGATIVE REACTION

- You don't know where to look first.
- You see an object's color or pattern first, then the object itself.
- The room is not balanced (i.e., the overall composition doesn't create a harmonious ensemble).
- The room lacks personality.
- One item dominates the room.

If you find yourself looking at items within the room as separate entities rather than as integral parts of an ensemble, this needs to be remedied. All elements in a design concept need to work together. If the elements of the room's decor don't coordinate, you need to spend some time to determine why.

The important thing is not to give up. Many times it is an easy process to correct the problem. I suggest moving furnishings and accessories and consider adding or removing items. The smallest of details can have a big impact on the final result, as you have already learned. Above all, don't feel bad if your design needs a little tweaking. All good designers continue to refine and make changes after the original concept has been developed and implemented. In fact, the most-used item for the best artists and interior designers is an eraser! So take heart—with just a little more effort you will be basking in the glory of a completed, professional-looking interior decor.

ABOVE **This small sitting room combines periods and styles in the form of a nineteenth-century writing desk paired with contemporary upholstery and area rug.**

OPPOSITE **In this small foyer in my home, I used bold colors on the wall and in the custom console table that sits underneath a work by Paul Goodnight.**

POSITIVE REACTION

- Your eyes move easily from one item to the next.
- Items in the room seem to be connected visually and work together as an ensemble.
- The items in the room are balanced.

If you find yourself drawn in by the decor—you know you love it, but you can't settle on any one reason why—then you've done your homework and all of your hard work has been worth it. Call your mother, call your friends, even call your co-workers. This is an impressive feat and should be celebrated accordingly!

Remember not to get discouraged if your finished decor is not everything you had hoped for. I suggest rereading the "Let's Review" sections at the end of each chapter to review the main points of each step. This may help pinpoint why an aspect of your design is not working.

① ② ③ ④ ⑤ ⑥ ⑦ ⑧

STEP
9

Let's Review

Now that you've completed your new interior design, it is time to evaluate how well you did it. But before you do, it's important to keep in mind that many of the decisions you made regarding the style of your home were affected by things other than your own taste. Factors that will determine what your space looks like are: architectural features, how the room will be used, and principles of good interior design. If you can remember that not every decision was within your control, you will be more objective about your assessment of the finished result, and that will be important when you decide what needs to be changed, if anything.

Immediately before you make the final evaluation, I recommend that you leave the house for at least eight hours. During the time away from the house, don't think about your design; you want to clear your head as much as possible. Once you've done that, it's time to look at your space anew. If you have been successful at applying the information I have presented throughout the book, when you look at the room, you should see a balanced composition that your eyes move easily around—no one item stands out or dominates the room. If, however, you are in the room and you don't know where to look first, or the furnishings within the room don't work together as a harmonious ensemble, you may need to make some changes. This may be as simple as taking something away, or moving some furniture around. If in doubt, look through the book and study the pictures again and reread the Let's Review sections at the end of each step to make sure you have heeded my recommendations. Whatever you do, don't worry too much, because all the information you need to make a great design is provided for you—all you have to do is follow it!

Final Thoughts

THROUGHOUT THIS BOOK I have shown you hundreds of photos of my interior designs, and I hope that you have enjoyed looking at them and that they have inspired you. What I haven't been able to show you are my clients' reactions as they see their completed designs and savor the beauty and spirit of the newly decorated spaces for the first time.

For most of my career, I would design every aspect of a house while the client awaited the date of completion from a different location. I would order all the elements I needed and wait to install everything at the same time. When I was done, I felt strongly about not being at the "final reveal," as they say in TV. I believed that the first viewing was a private moment.

About five years ago a client insisted that Shea, my niece and office manager, and I be present when the family opened the front door for the first time. They also asked that we use their camera to video this special day.

I decided to go against my usual policy, and I am glad I did. Emotions were running high, and my client began crying as she walked around her house. I looked at her and asked, "Are those tears of joy or sadness?" She replied, "Joy, love, and happiness!"

I had always believed that interior design was important—I dedicated my life to it after all. But that moment was so impactful for both my client and me. It was a very powerful reminder that our immediate surroundings play an enormous role in how we feel. My sincere hope is that you are able to realize an interior design in your own home that elicits the same feelings of joy, love, and happiness.

RIGHT **I wanted to carry over the romantic feel of the rest of this house into the library/study, but with a distinctively masculine flavor. The room has a gracious, old-world opulence, which I created by using an embossed tray ceiling with gold finish, an ornately carved desk, and cabinetry in richly colored wood. To keep the proper color balance, I used upholstery in lighter colors, a neutral floor covering, and a contemporary glass side table.**

OPPOSITE **This Florida home always elicits "ooohs" and "aaahs" from first-time visitors—or so my client tells me! In the living room, beige and copper leather seating is framed and accented by metal wall treatments and large moldings made of Japanese ash. The contemporary art on the walls echoes the color scheme of copper, beige, silver, and black.**

Appendix:
Standard Furniture Sizes

I put the following information together based on years of experience, as well as extensive research. Additional information has been culled from the American Institute of Architects' *Architectural Standards* guide and various online sources. Be aware that furniture will often vary by a few inches for different manufacturers.

NOTE The dimensions listed here are standard sizes for most American manufacturers, and European sizes may vary somewhat. To convert these measurements to metric, multiply the number of inches by 2.54. For example, 12 inches equals 30.48 cm.

SEATING

The average seat height for a chair, sofa, or ottoman is about 18 inches above the floor. The average arm height is about 23 inches from the floor.

TYPE	WIDTH	DEPTH
Arm/club/lounge chair	25$\frac{1}{2}$"–40"	25$\frac{1}{2}$"–40"
Bench	30"–144"	15"–33"
Dining—armchair	18"–27"	19$\frac{1}{2}$"–32$\frac{1}{4}$"
Dining—side chair (armless)	16"–23$\frac{1}{2}$"	18$\frac{1}{2}$"–32$\frac{1}{4}$"
Ottoman	18"–48"	18"–38"
Recliner	36"	66"
Sofa/loveseat	48"–112"	28–37"

TABLES

TYPE	HEIGHT	LENGTH	WIDTH/DEPTH
Card	26"–30"	30"–36"	30"–36"
Coffee, round	15"–17"	36"–42" diam.	36"–42" diam.
Coffee, rectangular	15"–17"	36"–60"	18"–24"
Console	28"	48"–54"	16"–18"
Drum	30"	36" diam.	36" diam.
End, rectangular	17"–28"	21"–48"	19"–28"
End, square	17"–28"	15"–32"	15"–32"
End, round	18"–22"	16"–30" diam.	16"–30" diam.
Hallway/entry	34"–36"	36"–72"	16"–20"
Night (see Bedroom Furniture below)			
Sideboard	28"–30"	69"–79"	18–23"
Sofa (table)	26"–27"	60"	14"–17"
Writing	28"–30"	36"–40"	20"–24"

DINING TABLES

SEATING FOR	RECTANGULAR WIDTH	RECTANGULAR LENGTH	SQUARE WIDTH	ROUND DIAMETER
2	22"–28"	28"–32"	24"–30"	22"–28"
4	38"–36"	44"–52"	32"–42"	32"–42"
6	34"–42"	60"–72"	44"–52"	46"–54"
8	34"–42"	72"–90"	48"–54"	56"–72"
10	42"–48"	96"–108"	56"–62"	72"–84"

WALL UNITS

TYPE	WIDTH	DEPTH	HEIGHT
Armoires	48"–54"	24"–27"	60"–84"
Bookcase (freestanding)	24"–48"	8"–24"	30"–84"
Breakfront/buffet/china cabinet			
Base unit (only)	36"–48"	15"–25"	30"–36"
Display/hutch unit (top only)	36"–48"	10"–13"	36"–54"
Combined unit			72"–84"
Entertainment unit	92"–102"	32"	48"–84"

BEDROOM FURNITURE

TYPE	WIDTH	DEPTH	HEIGHT
Bed (see note below)			
Dresser (Bureau)	36"–48"	18"–24"	29"–37"
Chest of drawers	32"–40"	18"–22"	42"–56"
Double dresser	60"–72"	18"–22"	26"–34"
Night table	18"–28"	16"–22"	16"–25"
Blanket chest	32"–54"	14"–22"	16"–20"
Lingerie chest	22"–24"	16"–18"	50"–54"

It is impossible to develop a list of standard bed frame sizes because of the wide variety of styles available. Therefore, it is suggested that you use the mattress dimensions listed below to estimate the amount of space needed.

MATTRESS SIZES	WIDTH	LENGTH
Bunk	30"/33"	75"
Dorm/hospital single	36"	75"
Twin	39"	75"/80"/84"
Double	54"	75"/80"
Queen	60"	80"/84"
King	76"	80"/84"
California king	72"	84"

Mattresses are available in many different types, the most common of which are listed below. You may never need these depth measurements, but you should be aware that if your mattress is deeper than the standard, bed linens might not fit. It is also helpful to know the height from the floor to the top of your mattress or box spring when buying comforters, bedspreads, and dust ruffles.

MATTRESS TYPE	THICKNESS
Inner spring	$5^{1}/_{2}$"–$6^{1}/_{2}$"
Foam	4"–$7^{1}/_{2}$"
Box spring	$5^{1}/_{2}$"–9"
Futon	3"–6"

KITCHEN

Though not strictly furniture, cabinets and appliances are, nevertheless, staples in every home. If you are planning to remodel your kitchen, you should contact a licensed professional to assist you with the planning and implementation. However, I have listed here standard cabinet dimensions, as well as standard appliance sizes, for the purposes of planning and general information.

BASE CABINETS	MEASUREMENTS
Cabinet depth	24"
Countertop depth (1" overlap)	25"
Height from floor to countertop	36"

WALL CABINETS	MEASUREMENTS
Depth (25" deep countertop)	$12^{1}/_{4}$"
Depth (30" deep countertop)	15"
Height of cabinet above countertop	18"
Height of cabinet above stove top	24"
Width	to match base cabinet

APPLIANCE	WIDTH	DEPTH	HEIGHT
Cook top	12"–48"	18"–22"	2"–3"
Dishwasher	23"–24"	23"–26"	33"–35"
Microwave	21"–23"	14"–22"	13"–18"
Range	19"–40"	22"–28"	23"–68"
Range hood	24"–72"	12"–72"	5"–8"
Refrigerator	24"–36"	26"–33"	55"–69"
Trash compactor	33"–35"	18"–24"	33"–35"
Wall oven, single	21"–24"	21"–23"	23"–25"
Wall oven, double	21"–24"	21"–23"	39"–50"

These appliance dimensions are from American manufacturers. European appliances may differ substantially in size.

Sources

Below is a list of retailers and resources that may be helpful to you as you design your home. Of course, I strongly suggest that you also take the time to get to know what is available in your community. This gives you the opportunity to see the product for yourself before you buy it.

Cecil's Designers Unlimited
(What kind of designer would I be if I didn't recommend myself!)
6601 Lyons Road, Suite C4
Coconut Creek, FL 33073
(954) 570-5843 or visit
www.cecilhayes.com

DEPARTMENT STORES

Macy's (furnishings and home decor)
Visit www.macys.com

Target (affordable home decor)
Visit www.target.com

DESIGN CENTERS (OPEN TO THE PUBLIC)

Expo Design Center
Locations in Arizona, California, Florida, Georgia, Illinois, Massachusetts, Maryland, Missouri, New Jersey, New York, Tennessee, Texas, and Virginia
Visit www.expo.com

Nebraska Furniture Mart
(furniture, flooring, appliances, and electronics)
Locations in Omaha, Nebraska; Des Moines, Iowa; and Kansas City, Kansas
Visit www.nfm.com

Robb & Stucky Interiors
Locations in Arizona, Florida, and Texas
Visit www.robbstucky.com

FABRICS AND TRIMS

Boca Bargoons
(decorative fabric outlet)
Locations in Arizona, California, Colorado, Florida, Georgia, and Texas
Main location:
190 N.W. 20th Street
Boca Raton, FL 33431
(561) 392-5700 or visit
www.bocabargoons.com

Calico Corners (decorative fabric, furniture, and home decor)
(800) 213-6366 or visit
www.calicocorners.com

Decorator Fabrics, Inc. (large selection of decorative fabric and trims)
1249 Sterling Road
Dania, FL 33044
(954) 925-8685 or visit
www.decofab.com

Hancock Fabrics (decorative fabrics and trims, including Waverly)
Limited selection of upholstery-weight fabrics in stock; additional fabrics available by special order
Visit www.hancockfabrics.com

JoAnn's Fabrics & Crafts (decorative fabrics and trims, including Waverly)
Limited selection of upholstery-weight fabrics in stock; additional fabrics available by special order
Visit www.joann.com

Rag Shop (limited selection of decorative fabrics)
Stores in Connecticut, Florida, New Jersey, New York, and Pennsylvania
Visit www.ragshop.com

Vintage Fabrics & Etc. (vintage textiles and imported indigos)
3500 N.E. 11th Avenue, Suite C
Fort Lauderdale, FL 33334
(954) 564-4392

FURNISHINGS AND HOME DECOR

Ballard Designs (traditional furnishings)
(800) 536-7391 or visit
www.ballarddesigns.com

Crate & Barrel
(contemporary and transitional furnishings and home decor)
(800) 967-6696 or visit
www.crateandbarrel.com

Design Within Reach (contemporary furnishings and home decor)
(800) 944-2233 or visit www.dwr.com

Ethan Allen (traditional/transitional furnishings and home decor)
Visit www.ethanallen.com

Floridian Furniture
(urban/contemporary furnishings)
4797 S.W. 8th Street
Miami, FL 33134
(305) 448-2639

High Brow Furniture
(modern furniture catalog)
2110 8th Avenue South
Nashville, TN 37204
(888) 329-0219 or visit
www.highbrowfurniture.com

Land's End Home (the popular retailer now has a home division)
(800) 963-4816 or visit
www.landsend.com

La-Z-Boy (recliners are back—and they are spectacular!)
Available at retail locations nationwide or visit www.lazboy.com

Cecil's Signature Furniture Collection for Mikala, Inc.
(handcrafted furnishings)
6601 Lyons Road, Suite C4
Coconut Creek, FL 33073
(954) 570-5843 or visit
www.mikalainc.com or
www.cecilhayes.com

Pier 1 Imports (transitional furnishings and home decor)
(800) 245-4595 or visit
www.pier1.com

Pottery Barn (transitional and contemporary furnishings and home decor)
(888) 779-5176 or visit
www.potterybarn.com

Restoration Hardware
(traditional and retro hardware, furnishings, and home decor)
(800) 762-1005 or visit
www.restorationhardware.com

Room and Company
(modern furnishings catalog)
(888) 404-7666 or visit
www.roomandcompany.com

Thomasville (traditional/transitional furnishings and home decor)
(800) 225-0265 or visit
www.thomasville.com

West Elm (urban/modern furnishings and home decor)
Stores in California, Georgia, Illinois, New Jersey, New York, Oregon, Texas, and Virginia
(866) 937-8356 or visit
www.westelm.com

Williams-Sonoma Home (traditional furnishings and home decor)
(877) 812-6235 or visit
www.williamssonoma.com

FURNITURE PATTERNS

Get It Right! Furniture Patterns
(lifesize furniture templates to make arranging easier)
6601 Lyons Road, Suite C4
Coconut Creek, FL 33073
(954) 570-5843 or visit
www.cecilhayes.com

HARDWARE AND HOME IMPROVEMENT CENTERS

Home Depot
Visit www.homedepot.com

Lowe's Home Improvement Warehouse
Visit www.lowes.com

Restoration Hardware
(traditional and retro hardware, furnishings, and home decor)
(800) 762-1005 or visit
www.restorationhardware.com

LIGHTING

Shades of Light
(lighting, draperies, rugs, and paint)
4924 W. Broad Street
Richmond, VA 23230
(800) 262-6612 or visit
www.shadesoflight.com

Y-Lighting
(contemporary lighting catalog)
(866) 428-9289 or visit
www.y-lighting.com

PAINT AND WALLCOVERINGS

American Blinds, Wallpaper, and More
(the name says it all!)
Visit www.decoratetoday.com

Sherwin-Williams
(paint and wallpaper)
Visit www.sherwin-williams.com

WINDOW TREATMENTS

American Blinds, Wallpaper, and More
Visit www.decoratetoday.com

Hunter Douglas
(blinds and window treatments)
Visit www.hunterdouglas.com

TO THE TRADE

Some home decor items are only available to the trade, that is, to interior design professionals including architects, interior designers, contractors, and manufacturers. These products may then be available directly from the manufacturer or in retail stores and design centers. If you are interested in any of the companies listed below, please call them directly to find out where you can get their products.

Photo Credits

FABRIC

Kravet (fabrics and trims)
225 Central Avenue South
Bethpage, NY 11714
(516) 293-2000 or visit
www.kravet.com

Waverly (fabric, wallpaper,
and home decor)
Visit www.waverly.com

LEATHER

Edelman Leather
Teddy & Arthur Edelman Limited
80 Pickett District Road
New Milford, CT 06776
(800) 886-TEDY or visit
www.edelmanleather.com

TILE

Walker-Zanger (stone, glass,
and ceramic tile)
(877) 611-0199 or visit
www.walkerzanger.com

WINDOW TREATMENTS

Hart-Lines by Valerie
(custom drapery)
1059 S.W. 30th Avenue
Deerfield Beach, FL 33442
(954) 421-5252

DESIGN CENTERS

Please note that each design center has
its own policies and procedures regarding
public access and purchases. It is
suggested that you contact your nearest
design center directly for information.

CALIFORNIA

Laguna Design Center
23811 Aliso Creek Road
Laguna Niguel, CA 92677
(949) 643-2929

Pacific Design Center
8687 Melrose Avenue
West Hollywood, CA 90069
(310) 657-0800

San Francisco Design Center
2 Henry Adams Street, Suite 450
San Francisco, CA 94103
(415) 490-5800

FLORIDA

Design Center of the Americas (DCOTA)
1855 Griffin Road
Dania Beach, FL 33004
(954) 920-7997 or (800) 57-DCOTA

GEORGIA

Atlanta Decorative Arts Center
349 Peachtree Hills Avenue N.E.
Atlanta, GA 30305
(404) 231-1720

ILLINOIS

The Merchandise Mart
320 N. Wells
Chicago, IL 60654
(800) 677-6278

MASSACHUSETTS

Boston Design Center
One Design Center Place
Boston, MA 02210
(617) 338-5062

MICHIGAN

Michigan Design Center
1700 Stutz Drive
Troy, MI 48084
(248) 649-4772

MINNESOTA

International Market Square
275 Market Street
Minneapolis, MN 55405
(612) 338-6250

NEW YORK

New York Design Center
200 Lexington Avenue
New York, NY 10016
(212) 679-9500

OHIO

Ohio Design Centre
23533 Mercantile Road
Beachwood, OH 44122
(216) 831-1245
(marketing office)

PENNSYLVANIA

Marketplace Design Center
2400 Market Street
Philadelphia, PA 19103
(215) 561-5000

TEXAS

Decorative Center Dallas
1617 Hi Line
Dallas, TX 75207
(214) 698-1300

Decorative Center of Houston
5120 Woodway Drive
Houston, TX 77056
(713) 961-9292

WASHINGTON

Seattle Design Center
5701 Sixth Avenue South
Seattle, WA 98108
(800) 497-7997

WASHINGTON, D.C.

Washington Design Center
300 D Street, S.W.
Washington, D.C. 20024
(800) 677-6278

Key: top (t), bottom (b), right (r), left
(l), bottom right (br), bottom left (bl)

Edelman Leather: 120 (r)

Dan Forer: 2–3, 6, 9, 12, 14, 17–18,
20 (b), 21–22, 26–27, 29–31, 32 (b),
38, 39 (b), 41(b), 48, 50, 54–55,
57, 59, 63–65, 66 (bl), 68, 72, 83,
87–88, 90, 92, 95 (b), 96, 100–101,
108, 114, 118–119, 124, 131, 145,
148 (b), 150, 152–154, 157, 160,
162–163, 170

Hart-Lines: 91

Lucia Herrera: 28, 43, 46–47, 77 (r),
84 (l), 112–113, 121, 123, 125–126,
128–129 (fabrics only), 139

Kravet: 45

Joseph Lapeyra/Dan Forer: 116

Keith Major: author photo on back flap

Mary Nichols: 102

Liz Ordoñez: 36, 146

Roy Quesada: 4 (detail), 16, 41 (t),
56, 62, 85, 148 (detail; t), 156 (t)

Kim Sargent Architectural
Photography: 1, 10–11, 19, 20 (t),
23–25, 32 (t), 33, 35, 39 (t), 40, 42
(r), 53, 58, 60, 61, 66 (t and br), 70,
77 (l), 80, 82, 98, 103–107, 110,
115, 117, 128–129, 138, 140, 142,
147, 149, 151, 155, 156 (b), 158,
166–169, 171

Sherwin-Williams: 73–76, 81, 84 (r),
94, 95 (t), 144

Walker-Zanger: 44, 120 (l)

Waverly: 13, 42 (l), 78–79, 86, 89,
132–137, 164–165

ABOUT THE PHOTOGRAPHERS

Dan Forer is an internationally
renowned photographer specializing
in architecture and interiors. His
work—which has included photographs of the homes of Sophia Loren,
Cher, Claudette Colbert, Wesley
Snipes, Sylvester Stallone, and entre-
preneur Richard Branson, among
others—has appeared in major
design publications, such as *Interior
Design, Architectural Record*, and
Architectural Digest.

Lucia Herrera is a graduate of the
Art Institute of Fort Lauderdale.
Specializing in fine art and architec-
tural photography, she is a seasoned
traveler and is currently based in
South America.

Native New York photographer
Keith Major has photographed
luminary personalities for more than
15 years. His client list includes
Sony Music, L'Oreal Cosmetics, and
Essence Communications.

Mary E. Nichols is a California-based
photographer who has captured interiors for *Architectural Digest* for almost
25 years. Specializing in architectural
photography, she has traveled world-
wide and shot homes as diverse as
Saudi Arabian palaces, Tuscan villas,
and contemporary California mansions.

Liz Ordoñez, a native of Honduras,
specializes in capturing the unique
quality of luxury homes. Her images
have been seen in architecture and
design magazines throughout the
U.S. and abroad.

Roy Quesada is a photographer
based in South Florida specializing
in advertising, architectural, and fine
art photography.

Over his three-decade career, **Kim
Sargent** has established a reputation
as one of the country's foremost archi-
tectural photographers. His images
have been featured in such notable
publications as *Architectural Digest,
Art & Antiques, Interior Design, Florida
Design, Metropolitan Home, Florida
Architecture, Veranda*, and the *New
York Times Magazine*.

Index

Accent colors, 141
Accessories, 143–159
    floor, 144, 152–154
    on furnishings, 144, 158
    tabletop, 144, 148–152
    wall, 93, 144, 155–157
Acoustical issues, wallpaper and, 80
Arm reach, from sofa to table, 52
Art, 143–159
    tabletop, 144, 148–152
    wall, 93, 144, 155–157
Artistic look, crafty vs., 146–147
Assessment, of light levels, 16–25

Balance, color, 116, 122
Balancing, of furniture, 66–67
    and walls, 61–65
Bathroom lighting, 20–21
Bending, body space for, 57
Body, human, and space, 52–59, 61

Ceiling, as layer three, 71, 93–97
Coffee table accessories, 150–151
Collectibles, 144
Color(s), 111–125
    accent, 141
    control of, 130, 131
    neutral, 141
    solid, patterns with, 134–135
Color balance, 38, 115–116, 122
Color distribution, 115
Color flow, 38, 114
Color rules, 115–116
Color selection process, 116–124
Combining. See Mixing
Console accessories, 152
Control
    of color and shade, 130, 131
    of pattern size, 130, 132
Conversation areas, body space for, 56
Crafty look, vs. artistic, 146–147
Crown molding, 94–95, 97

Decorative items, and space, 61–67
Details, 42–43
Dimension, wallpaper and, 78
Dining, body space for, 58–59
Dining table accessories, 148–149
Display units, 73
Distribution, color, 115
Durability, wallpaper, 80

Editing, of Look Book, 48
Evaluation, of finished design, 161–169

Fabric(s)
    lead, 138–140
    patterns and textures of, 127–141
    upholstery, 120, 122–123
    wallpaper and, 80
Faux finishes, 81
Finished design, evaluation of, 161–169
Fixtures, light, 97
Floor
    accessories for, 144, 152–154
    color selection for, 116–120, 121
    as layer one, 71–72
Floor plan, 34–35, 48
Flow, design, 38
    color, 38, 114
Furniture
    accessories on, 144, 158
    balancing of, 61–65, 66–67
    styles of, 70–71
Furniture plan, 51–59

Human body, and space, 52–59, 61

Ideas, shopping for, 44–47
Inspiration, looking for, 38–47
Investment, decorating as, 44
Item, size of, and pattern size, 133

Kneeling, body space for, 57
Knowledge, of space, 15–35

Layers, decorating in, 69–97
Lead fabric, 138, 140
Leg space, 52
Light bulbs, types of, 18–19, 21, 23, 25
Light fixtures, 97
Light levels, assessment of, 16–25
Look, crafty vs. artistic, 146–147
Look Book, 37–49

Measuring, of room, 33
Mirrors, 83
Mixing
    of patterns and textures, 130–137, 138–141
    of styles and periods, 99–109
Molding
    crown, 94–95, 97
    wall, 83–85
Murals, 81

Neutral colors, 141
Night table accessories, 152

Organizing, of Look Book, 48–49

Paint, 75–76, 94
Paneling, wood, 82
Pattern(s)
    fabric, 127–141
    wallpaper and, 76, 77, 78, 79
Periods, styles and, mixing of, 99–109
Plan
    floor, 34–35, 48–49
    furniture, 51–59
Plants, 154

Reach, arm, from sofa to table, 52–55
Room
    Look Book sections for each, 48
    measuring of, 33
    use of, 30–32
Rules, color, 115–116

Seating, 71–72
    body space for, 52–55

Shopping for ideas, 44–47
Side table accessories, 152
Size
    item, and pattern size, 133
    pattern, control of, 130, 132, 133
Sofa, to table, arm reach from, 52–55
Solid colors, patterns and, 134–135
Space
    decorative items and, 61–67
    human body and, 52–59, 61
    knowledge of, 15–35
Specialty wallpaper, 80
Storage units, 73
Styles
    furniture, 70–71
    and periods, mixing of, 99–109

Table(s), 73
    sofa to, arm reach from, 52–55
Tabletops, items for, 144, 148–152
Textures, fabric, 127–141
Three-dimensional floor accessories, 154
Trends, 44
Trompe l'oeil, 81

Upholstery fabrics, 120, 122–123
Use of room, 30–32

Variety, fabric, 127–141
View, 26–29

Walk space, 52
Wallcoverings, 74–85, 124
Wall molding, 83–85
Wallpaper, 76–80
Walls
    balancing of furniture and, 61–65
    items for, 93, 144, 155–157
    as layer two, 71, 73–93
Windows, and walls, 86
Window treatments, 86–92, 124
Wood paneling, 82